Milk and Honey
AN ESL SERIES FOR ADULTS

BOOK ONE

Milk and Honey

AN ESL SERIES FOR ADULTS

Jean W. Bodman
Michael R. Lanzano

HARCOURT BRACE JOVANOVICH, INC.

NEW YORK   SAN DIEGO   CHICAGO   SAN FRANCISCO   ATLANTA
LONDON   SYDNEY   TORONTO

Cover and Illustrations by Mona Mark.

Copyright © 1981 by Harcourt Brace Jovanovich, Inc.

All rights reserved. No part of this publication may be reproduced or transmitted in any form or by any means, electronic or mechanical, including photocopy, recording, or any information storage and retrieval system, without permission in writing from the publisher.

Requests for permission to make copies of any part of the work should be mailed to: Permissions, Harcourt Brace Jovanovich, Inc., 757 Third Avenue, New York, NY 10017

Library of Congress Catalog Card Number: 80–82924

ISBN: 0-15-558781-1

Printed in the United States of America

Preface

Milk and Honey is a complete series for teaching English as a second language. Students are introduced to listening, speaking, reading, and writing skills and are given an opportunity to practice and refine them throughout the five textbooks and their accompanying workbooks. *Milk and Honey* takes students from minimal or no competence in English to the point where they can function easily in a wide variety of situations. Designed for adults and mature younger students, *Milk and Honey* uses stories and visual aids to present grammar and vocabulary that the students can use in their everyday lives.

We began writing *Milk and Honey* to meet a number of needs: (1) the need to present the grammatical forms of the language in such a natural setting that the meanings of the forms are clear; (2) the need to give students the opportunity to express their own feelings, ideas, and experiences in their new language; (3) the need to introduce ESL students to the richness and complexity of spoken English through the gradual introduction and exploration of register (levels of formality and informality) and language functions; (4) the need to present valuable information and to practice useful skills (coping skills) that will help students adapt to life in the United States; and (5) the need to accomplish the above through activities that allow students to interact maturely, to direct and assume control of their own learning, and to be supportive of each other.

Since the 1940s, the field of English as a second language has been dominated by materials that present language structures in a controlled and logically sequenced manner. In recent years, many of these structurally based materials have come under criticism because, in an attempt to simplify linguistic complexity, they have distorted the way American English is really used. Despite this failing, our experience with adult students suggests that a carefully written structural approach has certain distinct advantages. The most important of these is that adults, when given the opportunity to attend to the regularities of English structure, seem to benefit—on the intellectual as well as the psychological level—from having the language broken down and presented to them in simple units. Thus, we felt that we could not, and should not, completely abandon the structural approach to teaching ESL. Rather, we saw the need to introduce basic elements through a structural approach with careful attention to accurately portraying the realities of American speech.

This alone did not meet all our needs. Studying only the forms of English, we knew, would not necessarily help our students to understand and be able to give sympathy, express disagreement, accept and decline invitations, and so on. A great deal of work had been done in Europe in describing language functions—the way people behave and make others behave through language. The result of this work, the functional syllabus, offers a new approach to teaching ESL. Instead of focusing on a particular form and the various situations in which it can be used, a functional approach examines the range of possible utterances in a given situation. Where a structural syllabus might have the student practice using *should* to give advice, the functional syllabus examines the many ways American English speakers give advice. For example, a response to *I really feel sick* could range anywhere from *Have you thought about calling your doctor?* to *Go to the doctor!* Thus, a functional approach helps the ESL student understand the delicate linguistic rules that call for the use of one utterance rather than another in any given social situation.

The functional approach, too, we hasten to point out, has some drawbacks. Since utterances can be judged appropriate only with reference to the social, physical, and temporal contexts, students must be supplied with detailed samples of speech acts. This means presenting them with large chunks of language. But how then are we to establish meaning? How can a beginning student not only concentrate on meaning, forms, and pronunciation but also manipulate the complex functional rules?

Our choice has been to begin teaching ESL using a structural approach. Books One and Three focus on structure, and language functions are gradually introduced as students acquire the self-confidence to handle the complexity. Books Two and Four, on the other hand, focus on functions, reincorporating the structures learned in the preceding books. New structures are introduced in Books Two and Four only as they are required by the functions being taught. In Book Five, the structural and functional approaches are fused.

The social context of the dialogues presented in the five textbooks is established by introducing a cast of characters that we follow through the texts. Representing people of various ages, nationalities, occupations, and social classes, these characters are based on students of ours who, over the years, have become part of our lives. The characters arrive here with the dreams and fears that all immigrants and visitors share, hoping that the United States will be their "Land of Milk and Honey." The characters have a threefold purpose: to provide a realistic context within which the students can study and learn the language presented; to provide interest and motivation for learning; and to provide emotional support through the knowledge that generations of ESL students have undergone similar experiences and have come out on top. Our hope is that the students in your classes will recognize themselves and their friends in our characters, and smile when they find our characters expressing many of the feelings they had when they first came here.

We have designed *Milk and Honey* so that students will spend most of their class time actively engaged in speaking English. Short models and dialogues begin the lessons. The students are asked to note the significant items in these dialogues—structures or functions. They are then given a wide variety of activities, which move from highly controlled drills to free and real conversations. Students repeat, make choices, play games, ask and answer questions, role-play, and talk to each other. Some activities are to be directed by the teacher; however, most are designed for students working in small groups or pairs.

The workbooks are designed to practice writing and reading comprehension skills. Coping skills—such as those described in the Adult Performance Level Study—are presented and used as a basis for writing practice. (The APL study was begun in 1971 by the University of Texas at Austin to redefine adult literacy in nonacademic terms and to measure the proficiency of American adults in those competencies.) In essence, the workbooks prepare the students to read and write the English they have used orally in the texts.

As the artwork is an integral and important part of our material, we have worked closely with the artist to ensure that the overall design as well as the individual illustrations contribute to the clarity and understanding of the material and that they present nonverbal information gracefully and accurately.

The printed page can do only so much. Our text, any text, can come alive only in the hands of a good teacher and willing students. And while we're at it, why shouldn't we say it? We believe in the field of ESL, the talent and professionalism of its teachers, and the dignity and intelligence of its students. We hope our work is worthy of them.

JEAN W. BODMAN
MICHAEL R. LANZANO

Acknowledgments

We would sincerely like to thank old friends, mentors, and teachers who have been so important to our professional lives.

Our teachers must include Joos, Coulthard, Wilkins, and van Ek who have reminded us yet again that we use language not as an end in itself but to accomplish certain tasks. Van Ek's *The Threshold Level for Modern Learning in Schools* (Longmans), was especially helpful in preparing this series. To Dr. Caleb Gattegno, we give our thanks for helping us become more aware of how we choose to use our students' time.

In the category of mentors, we must include Dr. Virginia French Allen who many years ago at Columbia University helped us understand that a language cannot be understood apart from the culture that produces it. We are indebted to Dr. John Fanselow who made us aware of the importance of focusing the students' attention on what is to be learned while providing a variety of learning activities. And we thank Dr. Earl Stevik for his gentle voice and his insistence that our students are people whose nonlinguistic needs must be acknowledged and accommodated if optimum learning is to take place.

Finally, we acknowledge our debt to our peers. Those late-night discussions, teachers' room arguments, and convention brawls were not just an excuse to have a cup of coffee or a beer. We were listening.

Contents*

		STRUCTURAL	FUNCTIONAL	PAGE
1	**People and Places**	PRESENT TENSE: Be I, you, he, she my, your, his, her what, where this, that from the	Asking, reporting factual information Identifying Introducing, responding to introductions	1
2	**Money, Money, Money, Money**	PRESENT TENSE: BASE FORM NOUNS: SINGULAR AND PLURAL how much, how many any, many, only and a	Correcting factual information	12
3	**Is Your Family Here with You?**	they NOUNS: IRREGULAR PLURAL WORD ORDER: NOUN + NOUN how old, who with, in but an	Socializing about one's family	23

* This table of contents combines a list of structures and language functions and the chapters in which they are *first* introduced and explicitly taught or practiced.

		STRUCTURAL	FUNCTIONAL	PAGE
4	Eyes and Size	PRESENT TENSE: BASE FORM + s/es WORD ORDER: ADJECTIVE + NOUN, ADVERB + ADJECTIVE how tall, what language, what kind of + NOUN very, very much, a lot	Expressing approval Asking about, expressing liking	31
5	How Much Do Jeans Cost?	VERB + INFINITIVE one some about, anywhere from ___ to ___	Expressing need Expressing desire	41
6	Two Blocks, Straight Ahead	IMPERATIVE NOUNS: POSSESSIVE FORMS there + Be me, it, them mine, yours how far, how these, those on, between, on the corner of	Giving directions Warning Expressing willingness Expressing and responding to thanks Saying goodbye	54
7	Citizens of the World	(Story introduction)	Socializing with strangers	71
8	What Are You Doing After Class?	PRESENT PROGRESSIVE: PRESENT, FUTURE Would you like to + BASE FORM Can + BASE FORM when, how about, how to	Expressing intention Inviting Accepting, declining, confirming invitations Expressing sympathy	76
9	Where Were You When I Called?	PAST TENSE: Be, REGULAR VERBS what time TIME CLAUSE: when in, from, at, on	Expressing disagreement Expressing displeasure	91

		STRUCTURAL	FUNCTIONAL	PAGE
10	She Turned on the TV and Fell Asleep	PAST TENSE: IRREGULAR VERBS why PURPOSE PHRASE: for + NOUN PURPOSE CLAUSE: to + BASE FORM	Asking, expressing pleasure Expressing homesickness	105
11	What Do I Have to Do to Learn English?	Have to + BASE FORM COMPARATIVES: er, more ___ than TIME CLAUSE: before REASON CLAUSE: because a ___ of ___	Expressing obligation Asking, reporting reason for feelings, activities	118
12	No Loitering	Get + THIRD FORM no + NOUN, no + BASE FORM + ing INCLUDED CLAUSES: how, where all of, most of, no one first, then	Asking, expressing opinions Expressing concern Expressing happiness	131
13	He Won't Eat Carrots	FUTURE TENSE: will + BASE FORM, Be + going to + BASE FORM CONDITIONAL CLAUSE: NON-PAST	Expressing fear	150

14	I'm Talking to Myself More These Days	PAST PROGRESSIVE
		  myself, himself, herself, themselves
		TIME CLAUSE: while
		SUPERLATIVES: the ___est,
		  the most ___
		too
		so
			Asking about, narrating a series of events	164

15	We Should Go Out and Celebrate	Should + BASE FORM Used to + BASE FORM	Advising others to do something Expressing enthusiasm	179

LIST OF IRREGULAR VERBS   189

Introduction

Each chapter of *Milk and Honey, Book One,* has similar elements. To provide variety, however, these elements are not always presented in the same order. In each chapter, we have included those activities we feel give students the most helpful and interesting learning experiences.

HOW TO SAY IT

In this section, a short dialogue is illustrated. Most teachers will find that students benefit most by having their books open, so that they can follow along as the teacher reads the dialogue. Teachers should try to anticipate the words or phrases their students might not understand and bring pictures of objects to class to help establish their meanings. More elaborate preparation should only be necessary for students who know absolutely no English and who are just beginning their work with this text.

The *How to Say It* section should take very little class time. The students should listen to the rhythm of the language and look at the illustrations and words. After hearing the dialogue read by the teacher once or twice, the students can then be invited to relax, close their eyes, and just listen to the flow of the language. The teacher should speak normally and not overenunciate. While it may seem reasonable in the classroom, such exaggeration will not help students understand people in the community outside.

DID YOU NOTICE?

The teacher should draw the students' attention to the information provided in the box. Students can be given a few moments to study the grammar and be encouraged to look back at the dialogue for an example. There is no need to explain the grammar further, as long explanations are not usually helpful. And while translations into the students' languages can allay some frustration and anxiety, a number of the items that appear in this section defy direct translation. Many teachers, therefore, elect to accustom the students to learning the language directly.

PRACTICE SAYING . . .

In this section, the teacher can now conduct a repetition drill. The teacher can say the sentence and then ask the students to repeat it. Individual students can be selected to say the sentence, while the teacher listens and helps the student correct any errors. Or the students can work with each other, the more skilled students assisting those who need help. This section does not contain all the sentences in the dialogue. In Chapter 1, for example, there is no need for the students to learn to pronounce the names of the characters in the dialogue. Nor is there a need in Chapter 3 to have the students practice repeating the numbers they learned in Chapter 2. In order to save class time for more important exercises that follow, only new items and items that need emphasis are practiced in this section.

HOW ABOUT A LITTLE PRACTICE
HOW ABOUT A LITTLE MORE PRACTICE

This part of the lesson is labeled practice, because the students are given tasks that involve mainly language manipulation as opposed to language production. The students' attention should be directed to the model. They should then attempt the activity in practice groups. Each group can designate one student to be the "teacher." That student should lead the practice, making sure that all students in the group have a turn to practice. In some of the activities, students are asked to look at a group of scrambled words and rearrange them into phrases or sentences. After a chapter or two, teachers will find that some students become very inventive with these activities and attempt sentences of surprising complexity. More advanced students will ask to add words, and the teacher can choose to let them do so.

For some students, working with other students in pairs and groups is as foreign to them as the language they are learning. They are used to learning from an authoritarian teacher who dispenses rules, lists of words, and passages to be committed to memory. Thus, some students will be unwilling to work with other students who, they feel, know very little. Also, some students may feel that a number of small groups buzzing among themselves do not show the teacher the proper respect. Still others will find the whole procedure so bewildering on a cultural level that they simply do not know what to do. However, we still find small group work beneficial for a number of reasons: students who are reluctant to speak before the whole class will participate more freely in small groups; students will have more speaking and practice time in small groups; and since groups may be homogeneously formed (the more advanced students can work together) or be formed of a mix of students (more advanced students can become "teachers" for the slower students), the teacher can then move among the groups and give individual attention where needed. In the first few chapters, a pair or a small group of students can be selected to work before the rest of the class. At first, it is best to allow them to remain seated rather than to bring them forward to be on "display." The teacher can assist the pairs or the group where necessary. Another pair or group can then be selected. As the students become more at ease and are familiar with class procedures, they can be encouraged to turn to each other and practice on their own. The teacher can circulate among the groups and assist the students if they request or demonstrate that they need help. Small group work should move along at a snappy pace so that students will feel their time is well spent. It has been our experience with students from every part of the globe that given time and patience, they will find group work beneficial and enjoyable.

FOR TWO (OR MORE) STUDENTS: ASK AND ANSWER

This is an activity in which students have an opportunity to practice communicating. The teacher should encourage students to give fresh, accurate, and truthful answers. The teacher can check that they are doing so by asking follow-up questions. For example, the student who repeatedly answers the question "What did you do this weekend?" with "I went to the park," could be asked, "Both days?" or "What did you do there?" This kind of questioning stimulates more communication and checks to see that the student said what he or she intended.

LANGUAGE GAME

These activities are designed to be fun and include guessing games, memory games, concentration and listening games, and "spontaneous" sentence completions. Like all games, students should be given an opportunity to play them more than once, since they will play more inventively and successfully with practice. We have found that students tend to be very responsible in deciding when these activities have ceased providing them with useful practice. Thus, teachers can let the students decide how long they wish to continue this activity.

READ THIS WITH YOUR TEACHER

This portion of the lesson usually contains an extended dialogue or a short story. The purpose of this section is to give the students an opportunity to see the language they are learning in a fuller context. The teacher can read the dialogues out loud. Or, as the students progress through the book, they can silently read them on their own. There are many opportunities for the students to perform dialogues. Therefore, we do not recommend that this section be *performed*. Rather, it should provide a break from the intense listening and speaking activities that precede and follow.

STUDY THIS GRAMMAR
STUDY THIS VOCABULARY

This section brings together grammar presented over a number of pages or introduces new grammar and vocabulary. We recommend that this section be handled in a similar manner to the *Did You Notice* section.

FLIGHT 18

Beginning with Chapter 7 and appearing at end-of-chapter thereafter, we have provided extended stories and dialogues written in structurally controlled English. Students in intensive programs (studying ESL more than twelve hours a week) or participating in classes lasting more than two and one-half hours a day, can be assigned class time to read this section silently. Other students can be asked to read and study the dialogues before coming to class.

PLAY WITH THE DIALOGUE

Students should be encouraged to take different roles in the dialogue as the directions specify. The "Director" should act as the "teacher"—listening for pronunciation problems, planning how the action is to be "blocked out" (where people are to stand and how they are to move), and arranging for any necessary props (such as chairs, pictures, and so on.) Actually, poor "performers" often shine and become great "Directors."

The students should be allowed sufficient time to practice the dialogue before performing it for the class. When students are asked to make an adaptation of the dialogue, they can be encouraged to write down their changes first and to create a script. The teacher's role in this part of the lesson is to circulate among the groups and encourage the students by providing ideas and linguistic information.

USE THE ENGLISH YOU KNOW

In this section, students are given more freedom to innovate and to use the English they have already learned and practiced. Those who have a good deal of self-confidence will be outstanding in activities that require role-playing. Although slower students may appear to be participating less, they still benefit from the experience.

Over the years, some teachers have expressed their concern to us about the many errors that students make during these activities. Our advice is to hold students responsible for the grammar they have learned in previous lessons and to correct other errors selectively. The decision as to which error to spend time on should be based on the teacher's assessment of the frequency and seriousness of the error. For example, verb tenses, modal auxiliaries, and prepositions are certainly worth a moment or two of class time. Specialized idiomatic expressions and unusual grammatical constructions are best left to later study.

BEING YOURSELF

In this section, the students are asked to construct dialogues and conversations. This requires them to draw from past experiences and to communicate their own ideas and feelings.

EXTENDING YOUR VOCABULARY

This activity demands the most from the students. Not only are they encouraged to speak freely; they may also be required to speak about subjects that require them to learn and use new vocabulary. Most beginning-level ESL textbooks do not require students to speak in multisentence utterances, because the authors feel that students need to be prevented from making errors. Despite preventive efforts, students *will* make errors. We have found, however, that these errors diminish with practice and feedback. On the other hand, there are distinct psychological benefits for students having "really said something substantial," albeit incorrectly, in English. For some students, this activity will produce halting and awkward utterances at first. Eventually, however, students will learn a great deal from their efforts. Students' conversations can be tape recorded, transcribed by the teacher or by the whole class (and written on the board), and corrected by the group and the teacher. If more practice is desirable for this activity, the teacher can create a Cloze practice by transcribing the conversations and then deleting every fifth word. The next day, the students can be asked to write in the missing words, either working alone or cooperatively within small groups.

Clearly, each chapter contains extensive exercises. It is to be expected that not all of the exercises will be appropriate for a particular class of students. Some may be too easy, others too difficult; the former can be completed rapidly, and the latter can be eliminated or given extra treatment. We leave it to your judgment to make the decisions—whether to continue to practice or to move on to a new activity. Students become discontented if they feel they are failing. Similarly, they are disappointed if too much class time is spent on things they feel they already know. Only the teacher can find the delicate balance between the two, which, when reached, will maximize learning possibilities. We, as instructors, expect a great deal of our students. We also have a great deal of faith in them, because it is our experience that adults can and do learn languages with great success. In writing this book, we have attempted to make the teacher's job easier by providing a wide variety of activities. It is for you, the teacher, to determine whether or not we have achieved this goal.

1 People and Places

How to Say It

Did you notice?

What	is
What's	

←a contraction

Practice saying this sentence.

What's your name?

For two students: ask and answer.

Student 1: What's your name?
Student 2: _____

1

How to Say It

> WHAT'S HIS NAME?
> THAT'S MR. CHASE.

> WHAT'S HER NAME?
> THAT'S MRS. GUTIERREZ.

Did you notice?

1.

MR. CHASE

MRS. GUTIERREZ

his name   **her** name

2. | That | is |
   |------|----|
   | That's | |

   ←a contraction

2

Practice saying these sentences.

What's his name?
What's her name?

For two students: ask and answer.

Student 1: (pointing to Student 3) What's _____ name?
Student 2: That's _____.

Read this dialogue with your teacher.

Carmen: What's his name?
Pierre: I don't know.

Pierre: Excuse me. My name's Pierre. Pierre Duval.
Karim: Nice to meet you, Pierre. I'm Karim Radwan.

Pierre: Carmen!

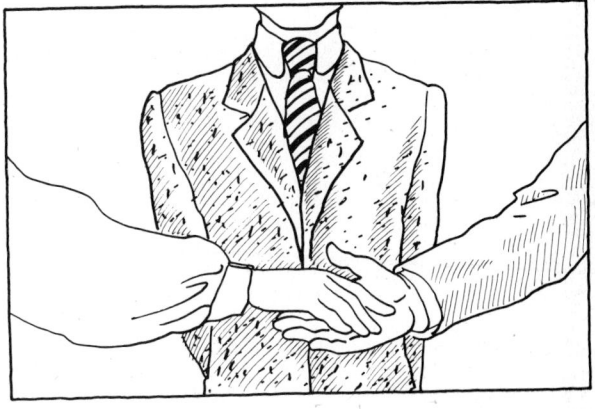

Pierre: Carmen, this is Karim Radwan. Karim, this is Carmen Lopez.
Carmen: Hello.
Karim: Nice to meet you, Carmen.

Did you notice?

1. "THIS IS CARMEN." / "THAT'S CARMEN."

2. "I'M KARIM." / "MY NAME'S KARIM."

PRONOUN	POSSESSIVE ADJECTIVE
I	my

3.
I	am

I'm
← a contraction

4.

"WHAT'S YOUR NAME?"

"NICE TO MEET YOU."

PRONOUN	POSSESSIVE ADJECTIVE
you	your

How to Say It

INFORMAL

"KARIM, THIS IS JOSÉ DORADO. JOSÉ, THIS IS KARIM RADWAN."

"HELLO."

"HELLO."

Practice saying these sentences.

This is José.
Hello.

For three students: practice introductions.

Student 1: _____ , this is _____ .
_____ , this is _____ .
Student 2: _____
Student 3: _____

How to Say It

VERY FORMAL

> SENATOR, I'D LIKE TO INTRODUCE MR. SOO HO KIM.

> MR. KIM, SENATOR JOHNSON.

> IT'S A PLEASURE TO MEET YOU, SENATOR JOHNSON.

> THANK YOU, MR. KIM.

Practice saying these sentences.

I'd like to introduce Mr. Soo Ho Kim.
It's a pleasure to meet you.
Thank you, Mr. Kim.

Language Game: Meet the Leader

Example:

[Panel 1: A man holds a picture of Margaret Thatcher (thought bubble: "I'M MARGARET THATCHER.") while another man says: "MRS. THATCHER, I'D LIKE TO INTRODUCE KARIM RADWAN. KARIM, THIS IS MRS. THATCHER."]

[Panel 2: A person holding the Thatcher picture speaks to another man: "IT'S A PLEASURE TO MEET YOU, MRS. THATCHER." The other replies: "THANK YOU, MR. RADWAN."]

For three students: practice formal introductions. Use pictures of famous people (or Visual Aids #s 1–10).

Student 1: _____ , I'd like to introduce _____ .
_____ , this is _____ .
Student 2: It's a pleasure to meet you, _____ .
Student 3: Thank you, _____ .

Study these language functions.

	VERY FORMAL → → → →		INFORMAL
INTRODUCING	Mr./Ms. _____, I'd like to introduce _____.	Mr./Ms. _____, this is _____.	_____, this is _____.
RESPONDING TO INTRODUCTIONS	It's an honor to meet you. or It's a pleasure to meet you.	It's nice to meet you. or Nice to meet you.	Hello. or Hi.
RESPONDING TO INTRODUCTIONS	Thank you, Mr./Ms. _____. or The pleasure is mine.	Nice to meet you, too.	Hello. or Hi.

How to Say It

WHERE'S HE FROM?

KARIM? HE'S FROM LEBANON.

AND WHERE'S SHE FROM?

MARIA'S FROM THE DOMINICAN REPUBLIC.

Did you notice?

1.

Where	is	He	is	Maria	is
Where's		He's		Maria's	

←contractions

8

2. Talking about countries

   Use the article **the** with the following countries:
   - the Bahamas
   - the Central African Republic
   - the Dominican Republic
   - the Ivory Coast
   - the Malagasy Republic
   - the Netherlands
   - the Philippines
   - the Sudan
   - the Union of Soviet Socialist Republics
     (or the Soviet Union)
   - the United Kingdom
   - the United States of America

   Other countries do not take **the** in front of their names.

   Examples: France
               India
               Mexico
               Panama

3.

STATEMENT			He	is	from	Lebanon.

QUESTION	Where	is	he		from?	

Practice saying these sentences.

Where's he from?
Where's she from?

How about a little practice?

Example:

[Illustration: Two men in foreground; one asks "WHERE'S HE FROM?" about a bald man with glasses. Reply: "MR. CHASE? HE'S FROM THE UNITED STATES."]

For two students: ask and answer.

1. Iqbal Singh/India

Student 1: Where's he from?
Student 2: _____? He's from _____.

2. Fusako Morita/Japan

Student 1: Where's _____?
Student 2: _____? She's from _____.

3. Francesca Bello/Italy

Student 1: _____?
Student 2: _____? _____.

4. Nikolai Popov/the U.S.S.R.

Student 1: _____?
Student 2: _____? _____.

How to Say It

> WHERE ARE YOU FROM?
> HOBOKEN, NEW JERSEY.
> JAPAN, AND YOU?

Did you notice?

STATEMENT		You	are	from	Japan.

QUESTION	Where	are	you		from?

Practice saying these sentences.

Where are you from?
And you?

For two students: ask and answer.

Student 1: Where are you from?
Student 2: _____. And you?
Student 1: _____

Study this grammar.

FULL FORM	I am	You are	He is	She is	We are	They are
CONTRACTION	I'm	You're	He's	She's	We're	They're

SUBJECT PRONOUN	I	you	he	she	we	they
POSSESSIVE ADJECTIVE	my	your	his	her	our	their

2 Money, Money, Money, Money

Study this grammar.

| QUESTION | | Are | you | | from | Poland? |

Language Game: Guess the Country

Example:

FUSAKO, ARE YOU FROM JAPAN?

YES.

MARIA, ARE YOU FROM VENEZUELA?

NO, THE DOMINICAN REPUBLIC.

For two students: ask and answer.
    Student 1:   Are you from _____ ?
    Student 2:   _____

Language Game: Guess the Name

Example:

For two students: ask and answer. Use pictures of famous people (or Visual Aids #s 1–10).

    Student 1:   (pointing to picture) Is that _____ ?
    Student 2:   _____

How to Say It

a penny    a nickel    a dime    a quarter

a dollar

Practice saying these phrases.

    a quarter   a nickel   a dollar   a dime   a penny

How to Say It

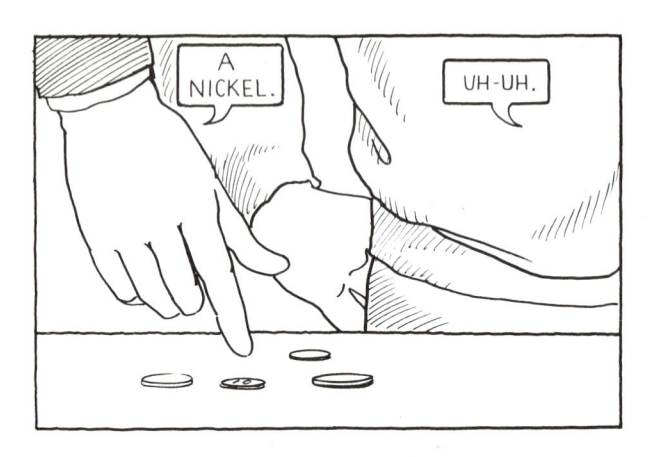

Practice saying these sentences.

A nickel.   Uh-uh. (No.)
A dime?   That's right.

How about a little practice?

Divide into small groups. Practice identifying the American money you have.

Study this vocabulary.

1 one   3 three   5 five   7 seven   9 nine
2 two   4 four   6 six   8 eight   10 ten

How to Say It

two dimes    four nickels    a penny

Did you notice?

SINGULAR	PLURAL
a dime a quarter	dimes quarters

Pronunciation Practice: practice saying the plural /z/.

1. dimes   2. nickels   3. quarters   4. dollars
   /z/   /z/   /z/   /z/

How about a little practice?

Examples:

a quarter

three nickels

Identify the money.

1.
2.
3.
4.
5.

How to Say It

two dimes and a nickel

a quarter and two nickels

15

Did you notice?

	+	
two dimes	and	a nickel

How about a little practice?

Identify the money.

1.

2.

3.

How about a little more practice?

Make phrases using these words and their plurals.

    a   four   dime   five   two   quarter   and   three   penny   six   dollar   nickel

Example: five dollars and a quarter

Study this vocabulary.

11 eleven	18 eighteen (8 teen)	30 thirty	100 a hundred
12 twelve	19 nineteen (9 teen)	40 forty (4 ty)	1000 a thousand
13 thirteen	20 twenty	50 fifty	
14 fourteen (4 teen)	21 twenty-one (20-1)	60 sixty (6 ty)	
15 fifteen	22 twenty-two (20-2)	70 seventy (7 ty)	
16 sixteen (6 teen)	23 twenty-three (20-3)	80 eighty (8 ty)	
17 seventeen (7 teen)		90 ninety (9 ty)	

Pronunciation Practice: practice saying these numbers.

thirteen	fifteen	seventeen	nineteen
(THIR-TEEN)	(FIF-TEEN)	(SEVEN-TEEN)	(NINE-TEEN)
thirty	fifty	seventy	ninety
(THIR-ty)	(FIF-ty)	(SEVEN-ty)	(NINE-ty)

fourteen	sixteen	eighteen
(FOUR-TEEN)	(SIX-TEEN)	(EIGHT-TEEN)
forty	sixty	eighty
(FOR-ty)	(SIX-ty)	(EIGHT-ty)

How to Say It

    1¢   one cent
  25¢   twenty-five cents
$11.20   eleven dollars and twenty cents

Did you notice?

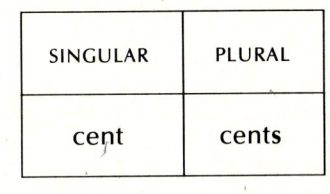

SINGULAR	PLURAL
cent	cents

Pronunciation Practice: practice saying the plural endings /s/ and /z/.

cents	dollars
/s/	/z/

How about a little practice?

Identify these amounts.

1. $20.98   _____ dollars and _____ cents
2. $15.95   _____
3.   67¢   _____
4. $2.53   _____
5.   99¢   _____

How to Say It

[Illustration: hand holding coins, "I HAVE FORTY CENTS."]

Practice saying this sentence.

I have forty cents.

How about a little practice?

Take out some change. Tell how much you have.

Student: I have _____ cents.

How to Say It

[Illustration: woman asking "HOW MUCH CHANGE DO YOU HAVE?" man replying "I HAVE FIFTY CENTS."]

Did you notice?

QUESTION	How much change	do	you	have?	
STATEMENT			I	have	fifty cents.

How to Say It

> HOW MANY NICKELS DO YOU HAVE?
> TWO.

> DO YOU HAVE ANY QUARTERS?
> NO, ONLY NICKELS.

Did you notice?

1.
QUESTION	How many nickels do you have?
ANSWER	Two.

2.
QUESTION	Do you have any quarters?
ANSWER	No, only nickels.

3.
any	+	PLURAL
any		quarters

Practice saying these sentences.

How many nickels do you have?
Do you have any quarters?
No, only nickels.

For two students: ask and answer.

Take out some change. Use these words: nickel, dime, penny, quarter.

Student 1: How many _____ do you have?
Student 2: _____

or

Student 1: Do you have any _____ ?
Student 2: _____

How to Say It

*Some Americans say "change of."

Practice saying these sentences.

    Do you have change for a dollar?
    Sorry, I don't.
    Thanks anyway.

For two students: ask and answer.

Use these words and their plurals.

a	quarter	five
dollar	nickel	ten

Student 1: Do you have change for _____?
Student 2: _____
Student 1: _____

20

How to Say It

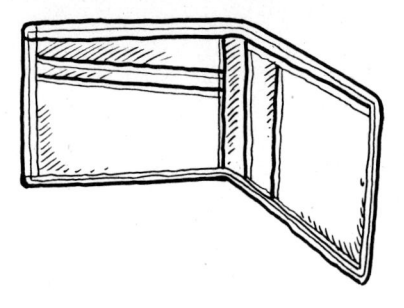

a wallet

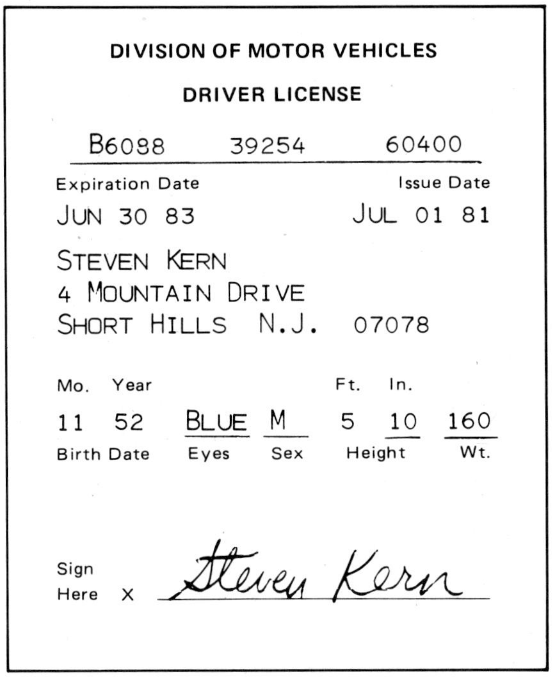

a key

a book

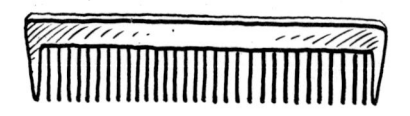

a comb

a picture

a brush

a coupon

a license

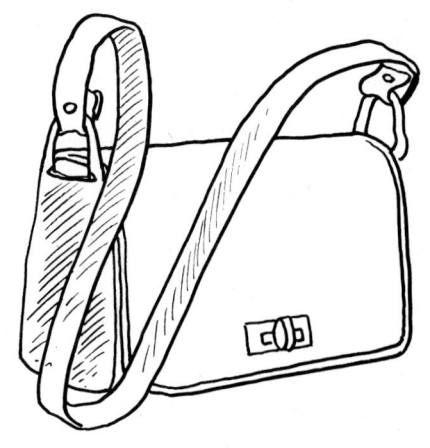

a purse

Practice saying these phrases.

a wallet	a license	a brush
a purse	a comb	a key
a book	a coupon	a picture

Pronunciation Practice: pronounce these plurals.

/s/	/z/	/ɪz/
wallets	keys	purses
cents	combs	licenses
books	pictures	brushes
	coupons	

Language Game: What's in Your Wallet? What's in Your Purse?

Example:

What's in your wallet or in your purse? Ask and answer questions. Use these phrases.

a book	any coupons
a brush	any keys
a comb	any pictures
a license	

Student 1: Do you have _____ ?
Student 2: _____

3 Is Your Family Here with You?

How to Say It

> DO YOU HAVE ANY BROTHERS AND SISTERS?
>
> YES, TWO BROTHERS AND ONE SISTER.

> DO YOU HAVE ANY BROTHERS AND SISTERS?
>
> NO, I DON'T.

Practice saying these sentences.

    Do you have any brothers and sisters?
    No, I don't.

For two students, ask and answer.

    Student 1:   Do you have any brothers and sisters?
    Student 2:   _____

How to Say It

Practice saying these sentences.

Are you married?
I'm single.
I'm married.
I'm divorced.
I'm separated.
I'm a widow. (female)
I'm a widower. (male)

For two students, ask and answer.

Student 1: Are you married?
Student 2: _____

Study this grammar.

SINGULAR	PLURAL
child	children

How to Say It

> DO YOU HAVE ANY CHILDREN?
> YES, TWO BOYS.
> HOW OLD ARE THEY?
> SEVEN AND FIVE.
>
> DO YOU HAVE ANY CHILDREN?
> NO, I DON'T.

Did you notice?

1. SUBJECT PRONOUNS

SINGULAR	PLURAL
he she	they

2.

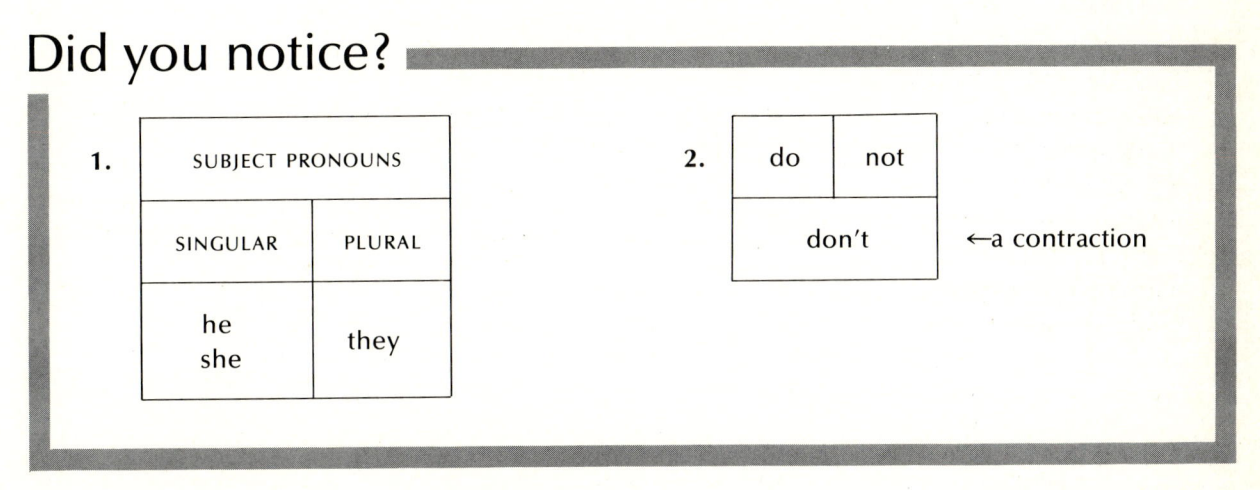

do	not
don't	

←a contraction

Practice saying these words and this sentence.

child   children
How old are they?

For two students: ask and answer.

Student 1: Do you have any children?
Student 2: No, _____.

    or

Student 1: Do you have any children?
Student 2: Yes, _____.
Student 1: How old are they?
Student 2: _____

How to Say It

(Panel 1) Is your family here with you? — No, they're in Lebanon.

(Panel 2) Is your family here with you? — My parents are, but my brother's in Rome.

Practice saying these sentences.

> Is your family here with you?
> No, they're in Lebanon.

For two students: ask and answer.

> Student 1: Is your family here with you?
> Student 2: _____

Study this grammar.

1.

+	AND	+
My parents are here	and	my brother's here.

+	BUT	−
My parents are here	but	my brother's in Rome.

2.

IN	COUNTRY
in	Lebanon
in	the United States

IN	CITY
in	Rome
in	Chicago

26

How to Say It

a book

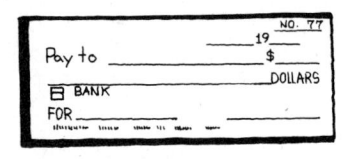

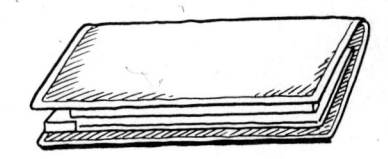

a check

a checkbook

a book

an address

an address book

Did you notice?

a + consonant
a book
a check

an + vowel
an address
an eraser

b c d
f g h
j k l   are **consonants**
m n p
q r s
t v w
x z

a
e
i   are **vowels**
o
u

y   is a **vowel** sometimes and a **consonant** sometimes

Practice saying these phrases.

a book   an address
a check   an address book
a checkbook

How about a little practice?

Example:

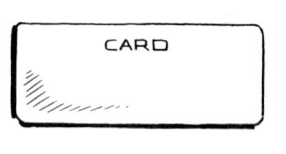

a card 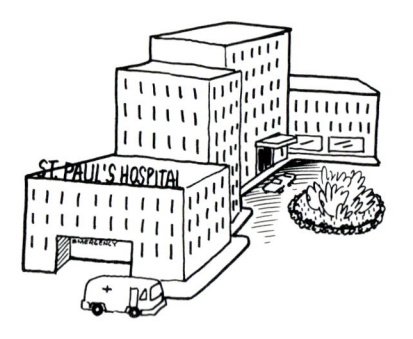   a hospital 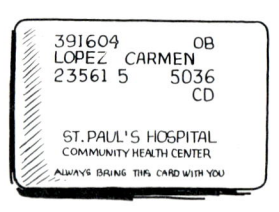   a hospital card

Make new phrases.

1.

a key    a house   _____

2.

_____   a mailbox   _____

3.

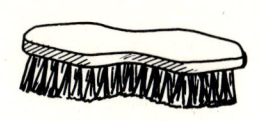

a brush   hair

4.

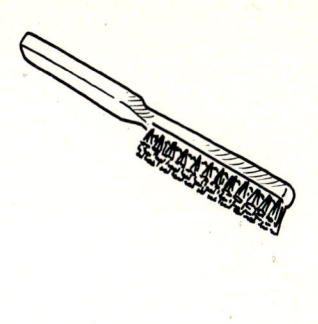

a bank

5.

a car

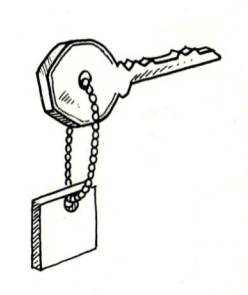

How about a little more practice?

Look at these phrases.

    a credit card   a bankbook
    a house key   a school ring

Now make new phrases. Use these words.

card	ring	book	key
hospital	wedding	bank	house
credit	key	school	car
social security	school	check	
		address	

How to Say It

How about a little practice?

For two students: ask and answer. In each question, use two or three words from this list.

ring	hospital	schedule	train
card	school	Blue Cross	draft
book	bus	registration	business
social security	library	car	map
identification	bank	credit	check

Student 1:   Do you have a/an _____ ?
Student 2:   _____

4 Eyes and Size

How to Say It

SHE HAS BROWN HAIR AND BROWN EYES.

HE HAS BLOND HAIR AND BLUE EYES.

Study this grammar.

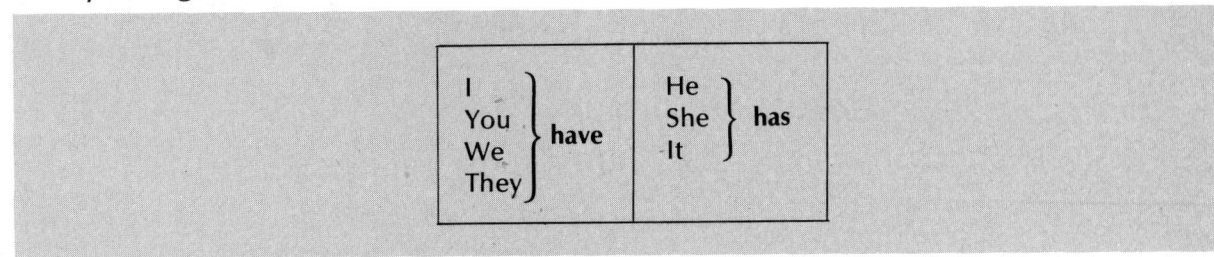

| I, You, We, They } have | He, She, It } has |

Study this vocabulary.

HAIR COLORS		EYE COLORS	
black	blond	black	green
brown	gray	brown	blue
auburn	white	hazel	gray
red			

Practice saying these sentences.

She has brown hair and brown eyes.
He has blond hair and blue eyes.

How about a little practice?

Example:

[Illustration: A woman with black hair standing; a man saying "SHE HAS BLACK HAIR AND BROWN EYES."]

Carmen Lopez
        Hair: black
        Eyes: brown

Describe these people.

1. Milton Chase   He has _____ hair and _____ eyes.
   Hair: brown
   Eyes: blue
2. Sophie Karkosza
   Hair: white
   Eyes: blue
3. Wen Yu
   Hair: black
   Eyes: black
4. Susan Gutierrez
   Hair: blond
   Eyes: green
5. Nikolai Popov
   Hair: gray
   Eyes: hazel

Language Game: The Mystery Student

Example:

[Speech: HE HAS BLACK HAIR AND BLACK EYES. HE'S FROM INDIA. / RIGHT! / IQBAL!]

One student describes a classmate. The other students try to guess his or her name.

Student: _____ hair and _____ eyes. _____ from _____.
Other Students: _____

How to Say It

[Speech: IQBAL'S VERY TALL. / NIKOLAI'S TALL. / PIERRE'S MEDIUM HEIGHT. / JOSÉ'S SHORT.]

Practice saying these phrases.

very tall   medium height   short

33

Study this information.

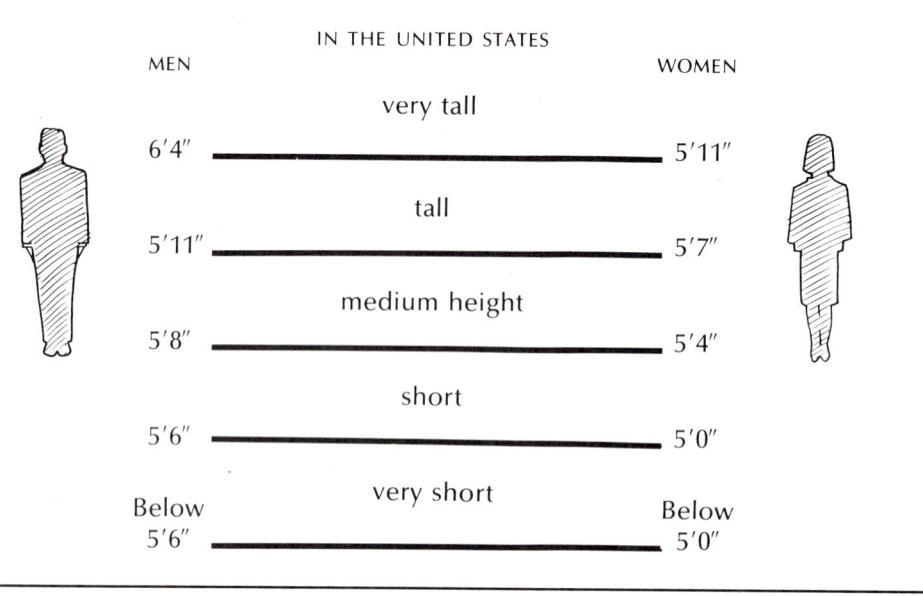

IN THE UNITED STATES

MEN		WOMEN
	very tall	
6'4"	———————————	5'11"
	tall	
5'11"	———————————	5'7"
	medium height	
5'8"	———————————	5'4"
	short	
5'6"	———————————	5'0"
	very short	
Below 5'6"	———————————	Below 5'0"

How about a little practice?

Make statements about your classmates. Use **very tall, tall, medium height, short,** and **very short.**

How to Say It

IQBAL'S SIX FEET, FIVE INCHES TALL.

IQBAL'S SIX, FIVE.

Did you notice?

SINGULAR	PLURAL
foot	feet

34

Practice saying these sentences.

He's six feet, five inches tall.
He's six, five.

How to Say It

Practice saying this sentence.

How tall are you?

For two students: ask and answer.

Student 1: How tall are you?
Student 2: _____

Read this dialogue with your teacher.

Susan Gutierrez: Is Jay here?
Milton Chase: Jay?
Susan Gutierrez: My husband.
Milton Chase: I don't know him. What does he look like?
Susan Gutierrez: He has brown hair and brown eyes. Medium height.
Milton Chase: Is that Jay over there?
Susan Gutierrez: Yes! Thanks.

Did you notice?

QUESTION	What	does	he	look like?	
STATEMENT			He	has	brown hair.

How about a little practice?

For two students: ask and answer. Use these words.

wife	mother	daughter	niece	aunt
husband	father	son	nephew	uncle

Student 1: What does your _____ look like?
Student 2: _____

Read this dialogue with your teacher.

Mr. Chase: Nice pictures!
Mr. Popov: Thank you.
Mr. Chase: Your family?
Mr. Popov: Yes.
Mr. Chase: Who's the blond girl?
Mr. Popov: My daughter Natasha.
Mr. Chase: Are those your sons?
Mr. Popov: Yes. That's Nikolai and that's Georgi.
Mr. Chase: They look like fine boys.
Mr. Popov: And this is my daughter Valentina.
Mr. Chase: A fine family, Mr. Popov. You're a lucky man.
Mr. Popov: Thank you.

Did you notice?

EXPRESSING APPROVAL

Nice pictures!
They look like fine boys.
A fine family.
You're a lucky man.

Study these examples.

Mr. Popov: I have a wife and four children.
Mrs. Karkosza: **How nice! You're a lucky man.**

Fusako: Do you have a girlfriend?
Iqbal: Yes, she's from India.
Fusako: **That's nice.**
Iqbal: She's here in the city.
Fusako: **That's good.**

Pierre: I have three girlfriends.
Karim: Three?
Pierre: Uh-huh.
Karim: **Good for you!**
Pierre: One's in Boston, one's in Chicago, and one's in New York.
Karim: **That's great!**

Practice saying these sentences.

Nice pictures!   Good for you!
That's nice.   You have a fine family.
How nice!   You're a lucky man.
That's good.   That's great!

How about a little practice?

Divide into groups of three or four. Show pictures of your families. Practice expressing approval.

Study this vocabulary.

COUNTRY	OFFICIAL LANGUAGE
England	English
Poland	Polish
Spain	Spanish
Sweden	Swedish
Turkey	Turkish
Germany	German
Italy	Italian
Laos	Laotian
Korea	Korean
Hungary	Hungarian
Norway	Norwegian
Russia	Russian
Portugal	Portuguese
Japan	Japanese
China	Chinese
Vietnam	Vietnamese
France	French
Greece	Greek
Thailand	Thai
Saudi Arabia	Arabic
the United States	English
Brazil	Portuguese
Colombia	Spanish
Canada	English, French
Belgium	French, Flemish
Israel	Hebrew, Arabic
the Philippines	Tagalog
India	Hindi
Iran	Farsi
Tanzania	Swahili
Haiti	French, Creole
the Netherlands	Dutch

How to Say It

> WHAT LANGUAGE DO THEY SPEAK IN HAITI?
>
> FRENCH AND CREOLE.

Practice saying this sentence.

What language do they speak in Haiti?

For two students: ask and answer.

Use the vocabulary on page 37.

Student 1: What language do they speak in _____?
Student 2: _____

Language Game: Guess the Language

Example:

> WHERE ARE YOU FROM?
>
> KOREA.
>
> THEN YOU SPEAK KOREAN, RIGHT?
>
> RIGHT. AND JAPANESE, TOO.
>
> REALLY? THAT'S GREAT.

For two students: ask and answer.

    Student 1:   Where are you from?
    Student 2:   _____
    Student 1:   Then you speak _____, right?
    Student 2:   _____

How to Say It

Practice saying these sentences.

What kind of food do you like?
American food.
Especially turkey and apple pie.

Study this Vocabulary.

AN INTERNATIONAL MENU

Italian	**Chinese**	**Japanese**
Fettuccine Alfredo	Peking Duck	Tempura
Veal Parmigiana	Pork Lo Mein	Sushi
Greek	**Spanish**	**French**
Moussaka	Paella	Coq au Vin
Arabic	Black Bean Soup	Bouillabaisse
Kebab	**Indian**	**American**
Humus	Lamb Curry	Roast Beef
Mexican	Mulligatawny Soup	Apple Pie
Chicken with Mole Poblano		Turkey
Enchiladas		

For two students, ask and answer.

    Student 1:   What kind of food do you like?
    Student 2:   _____. Especially _____.

39

How to Say It

[Comic: Man asks "DO YOU LIKE MUSIC?" Woman replies "YES, ESPECIALLY SPANISH MUSIC."]

[Comic: Man asks "DO YOU LIKE INDIAN MUSIC?" Woman: "NO. DO YOU?"]

[Comic: Man: "YES, A LOT." Woman: "OH."]

Did you notice?

I like music **very much.** = I like music **a lot.**

Practice saying these sentences.

Do you like music?
Yes, a lot.

Do you like Chinese music?
No, do you?
Yes. I like it very much.

How about a little practice?

For two students: ask and answer questions about music, movies, clothes, and food from different countries.

Student 1: What kind of _____ do you like?
Student 2: I like _____ .
Student 1: Do you like _____ ?
Student 2: _____

40

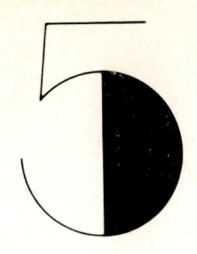

5 How Much Do Jeans Cost?

How to Say It

MRS. POPOV NEEDS A NEW PURSE.

Did you notice?

BASE FORM	BASE FORM + S
need	needs

Practice saying this sentence.

She needs a new purse.

41

How about a little practice?

Make statements about the following items.

1.

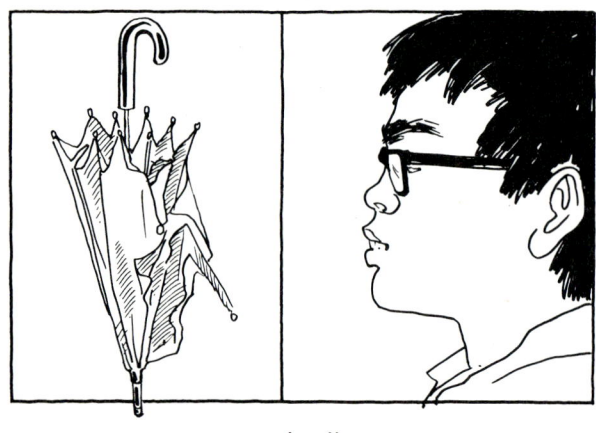

umbrella

He needs a new _____.

2.

sofa

3.

car

4.

comb

5.

coat

42

How to Say It

HE NEEDS TWO DIMES AND A NICKEL.

HE NEEDS A QUARTER.

How about a little practice?

1. He needs _____.

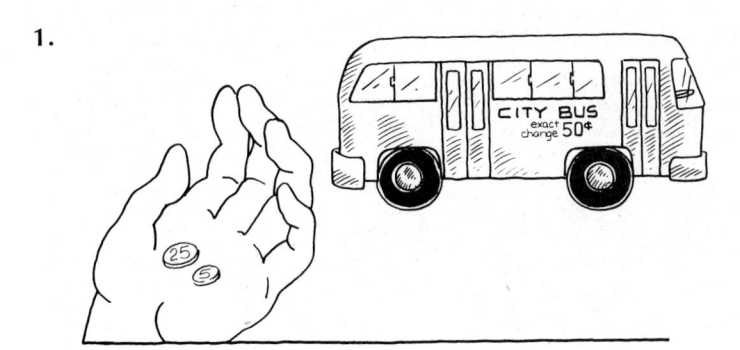

2.

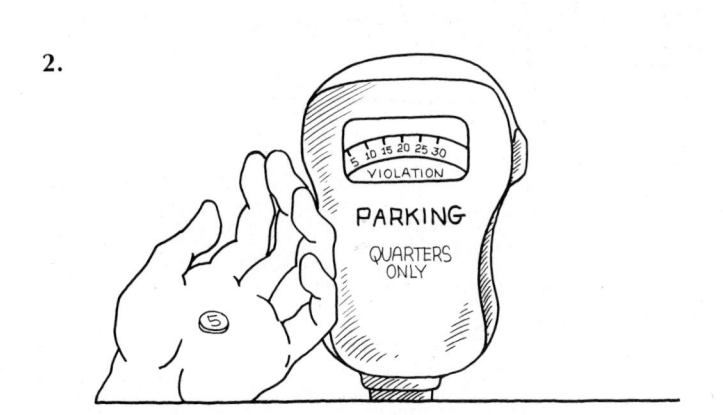

43

How to Say It

Did you notice the difference?

I need a car.
I need a new car.

Practice saying these sentences.

I need a car.
I need a new car.

Read this dialogue with your teacher.

Pierre: Maria, do you have a car?
Maria: No, we don't need one.
Pierre: How about you, Wen Yu? Do you have a car?
Wen Yu: Yes, but I need a new one.
Pierre: Oh?
Wen Yu: Do you have a car?
Pierre: Yes, a new Chevrolet.
Wen Yu: How do you like it?
Pierre: It's great!

Did you notice?

1. Do you have a **car**?
   Yes, but I need a new **one**.

NOUN	PRONOUN
car	one

2. I have a new Chevrolet.
   Do you like **it**?

NOUN PHRASE	PRONOUN
new Chevrolet	it

Study this vocabulary.

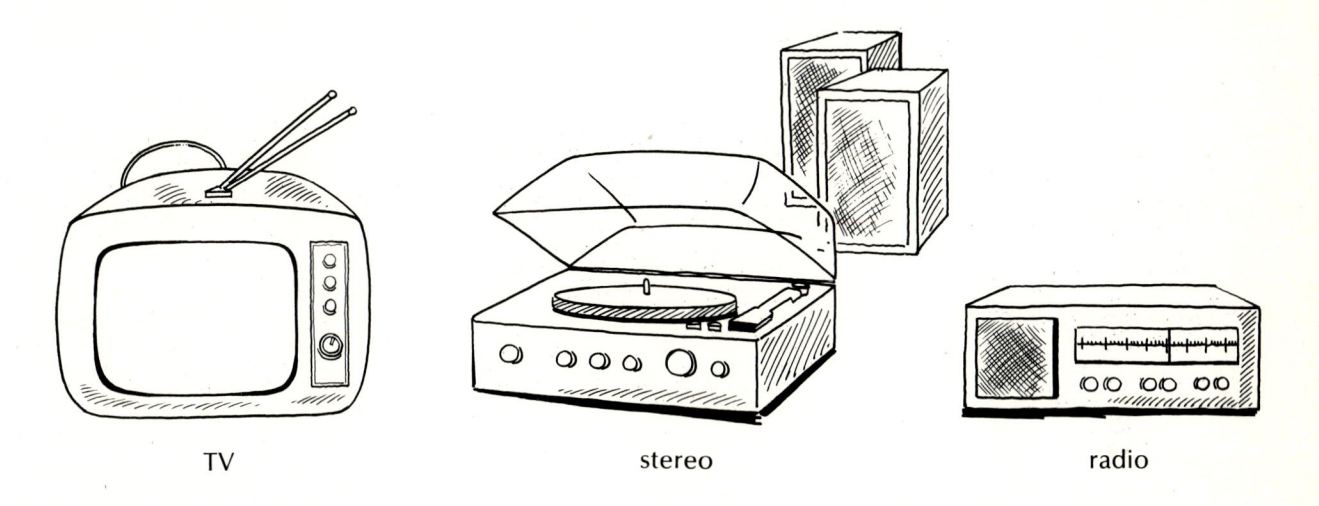

TV   stereo   radio

Practice saying these sentences.

Do you have a TV?
I need a new stereo.
I need a radio.
I have a new TV.
Do you like it?

For two students: ask and answer.

Use these words: TV, car, radio, stereo.

Student 1:   Do you have a _____ ?
Student 2:   _____

45

Study this vocabulary.

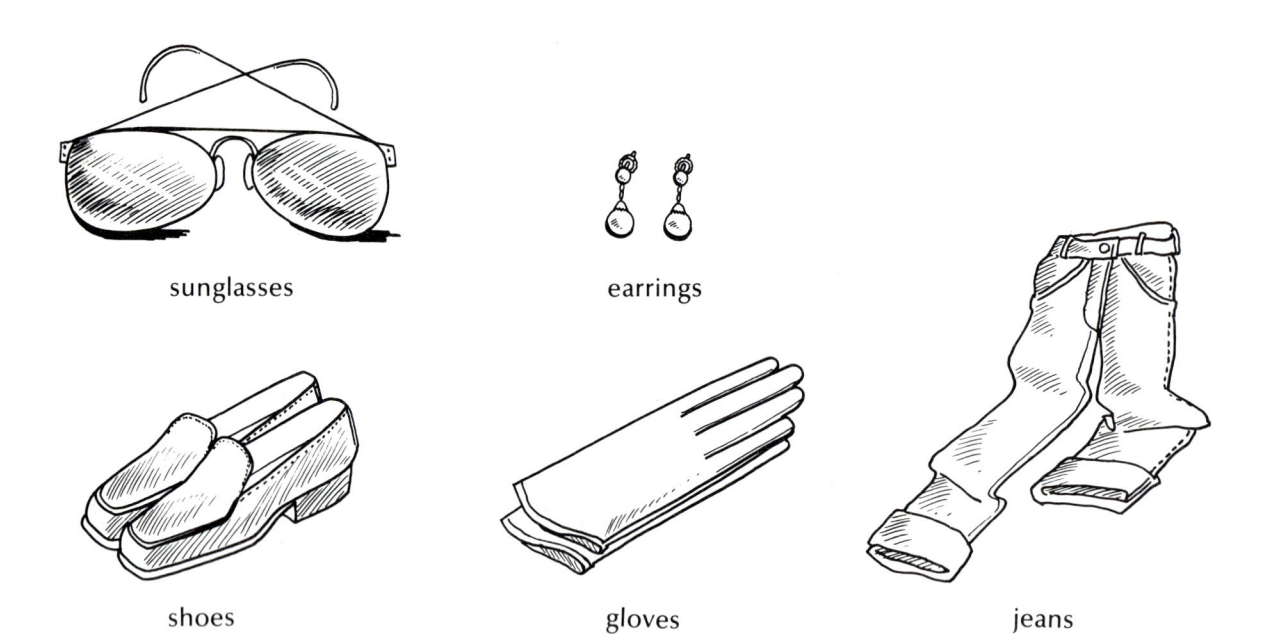

sunglasses

earrings

shoes

gloves

jeans

Pronunciation practice.

some shoes
/z/
some jeans
/z/

some gloves
/z/
some sunglasses
/ɪz/

some earrings
/z/

Study this grammar.

1.

SINGULAR	PLURAL
a **a** new car	some **some** new shoes

2.

SIMPLE PRESENT TENSE	
BASE FORM	BASE FORM + S
I you we they need	he she needs it

How about a little practice?

Example:

[illustration: three people with speech bubbles — "I NEED A CAR.", "I NEED SOME NEW SHOES.", "I NEED SOME JEANS."]

Make statements. Use these words.

shoes	car	TV	address book
stereo	gloves	jeans	pen
radio	sunglasses	earrings	purse

I need _____.

Read this dialogue with your teacher.

    José: Hey, Dad.
    Mr. Dorado: Yes?
    José: I need a hundred dollars.
    Mr. Dorado: What! What for?
    José: Some shoes.
    Mr. Dorado: A hundred dollars for shoes?
    José: I need some jeans too.
    Mr. Dorado: What's her name?
    José: What?
    Mr. Dorado: New shoes, new jeans. What's her name?
    José: Aw, Dad.

How to Say It

[Panel 1: "HOW MUCH DOES A TV COST?" — "ANYWHERE FROM $150 TO $500."]

[Panel 2: "HOW MUCH DO JEANS COST?" — "ABOUT $25."]

Did you notice?

			SINGULAR NOUN	
QUESTION STATEMENT	How much	**does**	a TV A TV	**cost?** **costs** from $150 to $500.
			PLURAL NOUN	
QUESTION STATEMENT	How much	**do**	jeans Jeans	**cost?** **cost** about $25.

Practice saying these sentences.

How much does a TV cost?
Anywhere from $150 to $500.
How much do jeans cost?
About $25.

For two students: ask and answer.

Use these words.

shoes	car	TV	wallet
stereo	gloves	jeans	driver's license
radio	sunglasses	purse	ballpoint pen

Student 1: How much _____ cost?
Student 2: I don't know.

      or

Student 2: About $_____ .
Student 1: Really?
Student 2: Yeah.

How to Say It

Soo Ho Kim

Soo Ho Kim **wants to buy** a desk. He **has** $125. The desk **costs** $175. He **needs** $50 more.

Did you notice?

1.

SIMPLE PRESENT TENSE	
BASE FORM	BASE FORM + s
want cost need *have *do	wants costs needs *has *does

* Irregular Verb

2. He **wants to buy** a desk.

BASE FORM + S	TO + BASE FORM
main verb	infinitive phrase

Practice saying these sentences.

 He wants a desk.
 He wants to buy a desk.

How about a little practice?

Look at the pictures. Make statements.

1. Carmen Lopez

Balance Forward	110	00
Deposits		
Total		
Amount of Check		
Balance		

Carmen wants to buy _____ . She has _____ .
The _____ costs _____ . She needs _____ .

2. Francesca Bello

Balance Forward	80	00
Deposits		
Total		
Amount of Check		
Balance		

Francesca wants _____ . She has _____ .
The _____ costs _____ . She needs _____ .

3. Soo Ho Kim

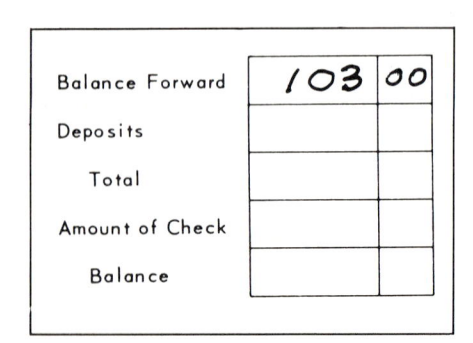

Balance Forward	103	00
Deposits		
Total		
Amount of Check		
Balance		

4. Pierre Duval

Balance Forward	230	00
Deposits		
Total		
Amount of Check		
Balance		

5. José Dorado

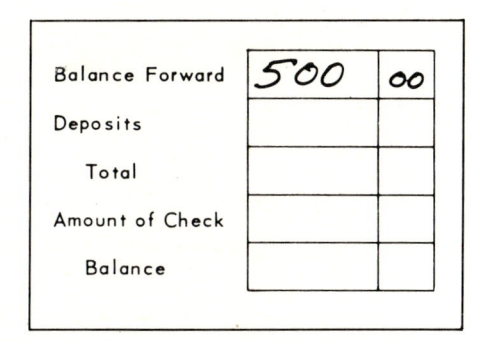

Balance Forward	500	00
Deposits		
Total		
Amount of Check		
Balance		

How to Say It

Practice saying this sentence.

He wants to see a movie.

How about a little practice?

Make statements.

1. Susan

go to a restaurant

Susan wants _____.

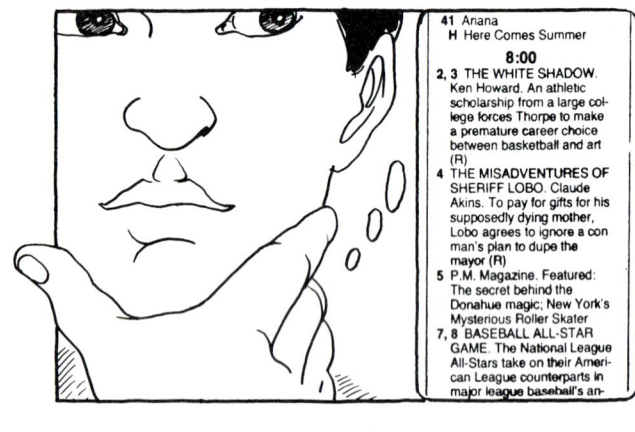

2. José

watch TV

José wants _____.

3. Karim

see some friends

4. Maria

go to the park

5.   Carmen

go shopping

Language Game: Playing with Words

Example:

"MY FAMILY WANTS TO GO TO A RESTAURANT."

"I WANT TO BUY A COAT."

"MY FRIEND WANTS TO GO TO THE PARK, BUT I WANT TO GO TO A MOVIE."

Make statements. Use words from this list.

buy	park	a	restaurant
TV	go	to	some
movie	my	friend	the
shopping	family	see	watch
learn	English	coat	shoes
I	want	and	but

53

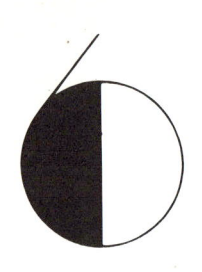

6 Two Blocks, Straight Ahead

Study these drawings.

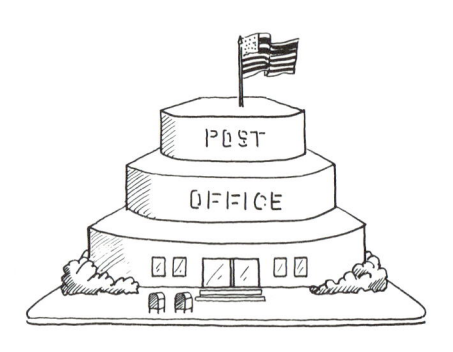

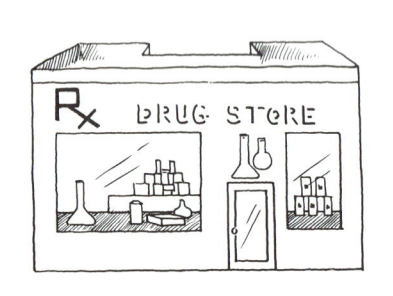

Practice saying these phrases.

a barber shop	a bank	a church
a gas station	a bakery	the police station
a dry cleaners	a beauty salon	the firehouse
a drugstore	a hardware store	the post office
a liquor store	the high school	a supermarket

How to Say It

Mr. Popov's car

the Chases' house

Francesca's stereo

Did you notice?

SINGULAR	PLURAL
's	s'
Mr. Chase's coat	the Chases' house

How about a little practice?

Give the names of these places.

Example: Al
Gas Station   Al's Gas Station

1. Kimball
   Department Store   _____

2. Carl
   Barber Shop   _____
3. Lorenzo
   Drugstore   _____
4. Alma
   Beauty Salon   _____
5. Singer
   Meats   _____
6. St. Mary
   Church   _____

Study this vocabulary.

a notebook   a dictionary   a bag

a pen   a ballpoint pen

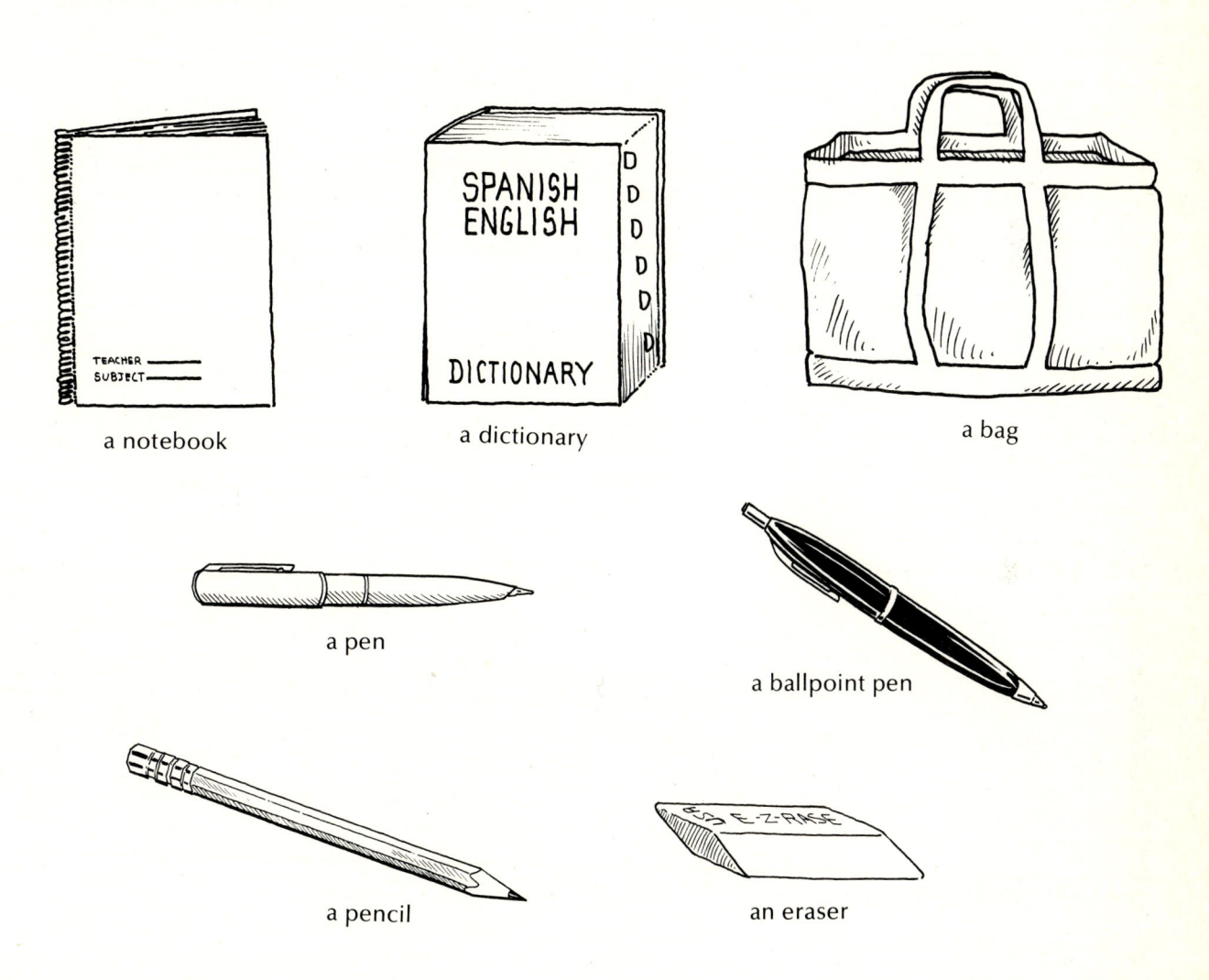

a pencil   an eraser

Practice saying these phrases.

a notebook   a pen
a ballpoint pen   an eraser
a dictionary   a pencil
a bag

57

How to Say It

[Panel 1: "GIVE ME YOUR DICTIONARY."]
[Panel 2: "SURE. HERE." / "THANKS." / "YOU'RE WELCOME."]

Did you notice?

IMPERATIVE
Give me your dictionary. ↑ base form of verb

Practice saying these sentences.

> Give me your dictionary.
> Sure. Here.
> Thanks.
> You're welcome.

For two students: practice using the imperative.

Use the vocabulary on page 57.

> Student 1: Give me _____.
> Student 2: _____.
> Student 1: Thanks.
> Student 2: _____.

How to Say It

> TAKE A DOLLAR AND GIVE IT TO JOSÉ.
>
> SURE.
>
> THEN TAKE THE WALLET AND GIVE IT TO PIERRE.
>
> OKAY. HERE, JOSÉ. HERE, PIERRE.

Did you notice?

Take **a** dollar.
↓
There are two.

Take **the** wallet.
↓
There is only one.

How about a little practice?

For two students: make commands. Use different objects.

Student 1: Take _____ and give _____ .
Student 2: _____ .
Student 1: Then _____ .
Student 2: _____ .

59

Read this with your teacher.

Study this grammar.

1. These are **my** pens. These are **mine**.
   These are **your** pens. These are **yours**.

POSSESSIVES			
ADJECTIVE	PRONOUN	ADJECTIVE	PRONOUN
my	mine	her	hers
your	yours	our	ours
his	his	their	theirs

61

2. **This** is your pencil. **These** are your pencils.
   That is your pencil. **Those** are your pencils.

SINGULAR	PLURAL
this	these
that	those

3. **I** need a pen.   Give **me** a pen.
   ↑   ↑
   SUBJECT PRONOUN   OBJECT PRONOUN

SUBJECT AND OBJECT PRONOUNS			
SUBJECT	OBJECT	SUBJECT	OBJECT
I	me	she	her
you	you	we	us
he	him	they	them

4. **Who** has a comb? Maria.
   Whose comb is this? Maria's.

INTERROGATIVES	
PRONOUN	POSSESSIVE ADJECTIVE
who	**whose** comb

Practice saying these imperative sentences.

Give me a book.   Stop!   Study this.
Pass me the bag.   Return everything.   Practice this.
Take this.   Listen.   Ask and answer.

Language Game: Pass It On

Example:

> GIVE ME SOMETHING OF YOURS.
>
> GIVE YOUR PEN TO SOMEONE, AND TAKE THIS BOOK AND PASS IT ON.
>
> WHOSE COMB AND BAG ARE THESE?
>
> PASS THEM BACK, PLEASE.

Practice giving commands.

Student 1, tell others to take different objects and to pass them on. Use the pronouns and adjectives shown on pp. 61–62.

Study these language functions.

	VERY FORMAL → → → →		INFORMAL
ASKING FOR SOMETHING	Excuse me, but would you mind handing me that book?	Could I have that book? or May I have that book?	Can I have that book? or Give me that book.
EXPRESSING POSSIBILITY/ WILLINGNESS	Of course. Here you are.	Sure, here.	Sure. or Here.
EXPRESSING THANKS	Thank you very much.	Thank you.	Thanks.
RESPONDING TO THANKS	You're welcome. or My pleasure.	Don't mention it.	Sure. Anytime. or Okay. or Uh-huh.

How about a little practice?

For two students: ask and answer. Practice using the expressions shown above. Ask for something, express willingness, express thanks, and respond to thanks.

Study these language functions.

	FORMAL → → →		INFORMAL
SAYING GOODBYE	Goodbye.	Goodbye.	Bye. or Bye-bye. or So long. or Take it easy. or See you.

Practice saying these warnings.

Watch out!   Be careful!   Don't move!
Duck!   Don't touch that!   Look out!

How about a little practice?

Example:

Look at the pictures. Give warnings.

1. 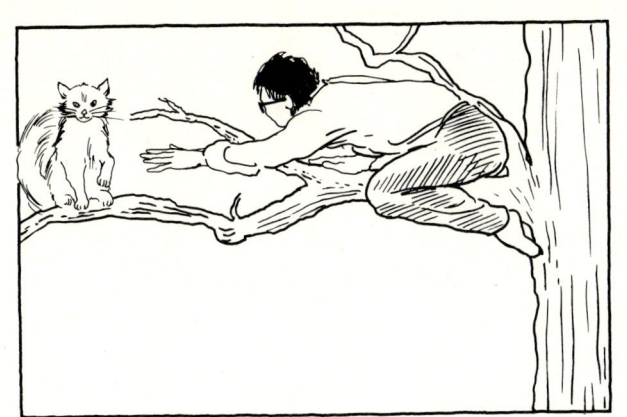
2. 
3. 
4.

How to Say It

"WHERE'S THE PUBLIC LIBRARY?"

"ON JOHNSON ROAD."

65

Look at this map.

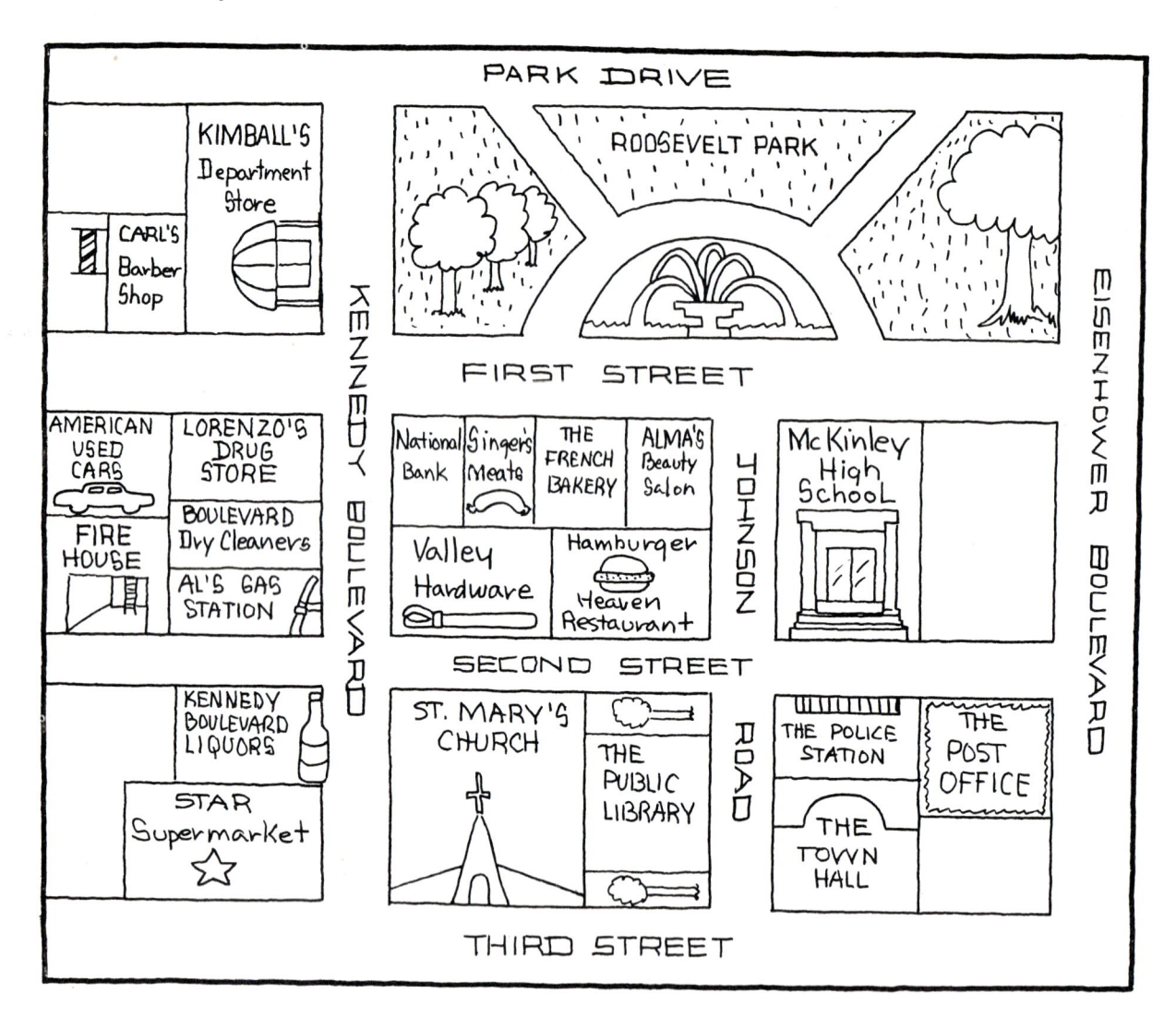

For two students: ask and answer questions about these places.

   The Public Library
   Singer's Meats
   The French Bakery
   Boulevard Dry Cleaners

Use the map on this page.

   Student 1:   Where's _____ ?
   Student 2:   On _____ .

How to Say It

Did you notice?

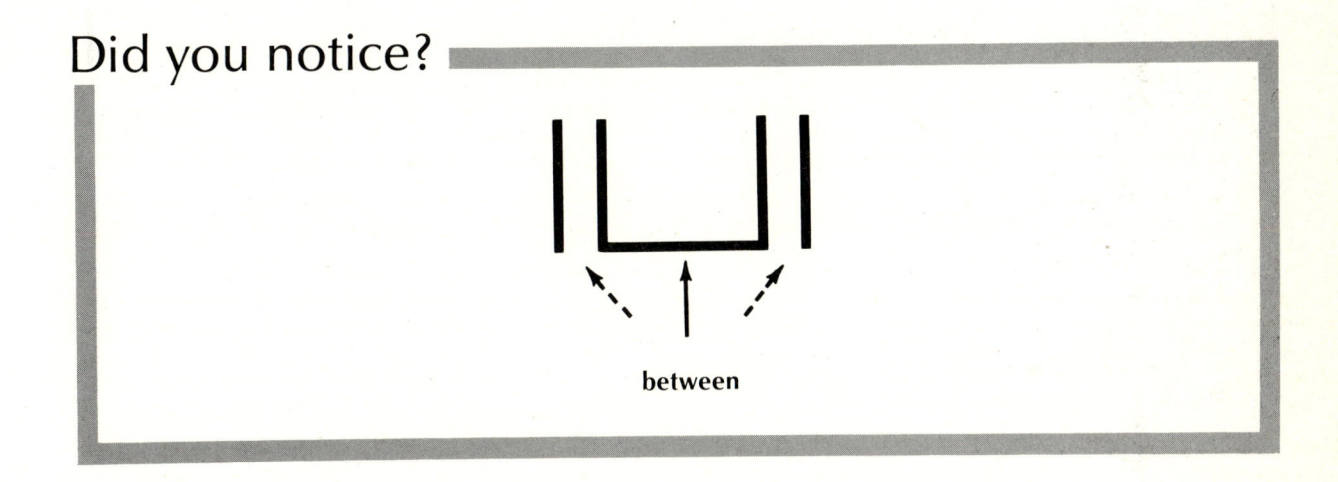

between

For two students: ask and answer questions about these places.

McKinley High School
St. Mary's Church
Roosevelt Park

Use the map on page 66.

Student 1: Where's _____?
Student 2: On _____ between _____ and _____.

How to Say It

[Illustration: A woman asks "WHERE'S THE POLICE STATION?" and receives the answer "ON THE CORNER OF SECOND STREET AND JOHNSON ROAD."]

Did you notice?

corner → ⌐

For two students: ask and answer questions about these places.

the National Bank	Lorenzo's Drugstore
the Post Office	Alma's Beauty Salon
Al's Gas Station	

Use the map on page 66.

Student 1: Where's _____ ?
Student 2: On the corner of _____ and _____ .

Read this dialogue with your teacher.

Look at the map on page 66 before you begin. José and Wen Yu are standing on the corner of Kennedy Boulevard and Third Street.

José: Is there a drugstore around here?
Wen Yu: Yes, on Kennedy.
José: How far on Kennedy?
Wen Yu: Two blocks, straight ahead.
José: Where's the Post Office?
Wen Yu: On Second Street.
José: Second Street?
Wen Yu: Go straight ahead, one block.
José: The Post Office is there?
Wen Yu: No. Turn right on Second. Go two blocks. The Post Office is on the corner of Second and Eisenhower.
José: Second and Eisenhower. Thanks a lot.
Wen Yu: Don't mention it.

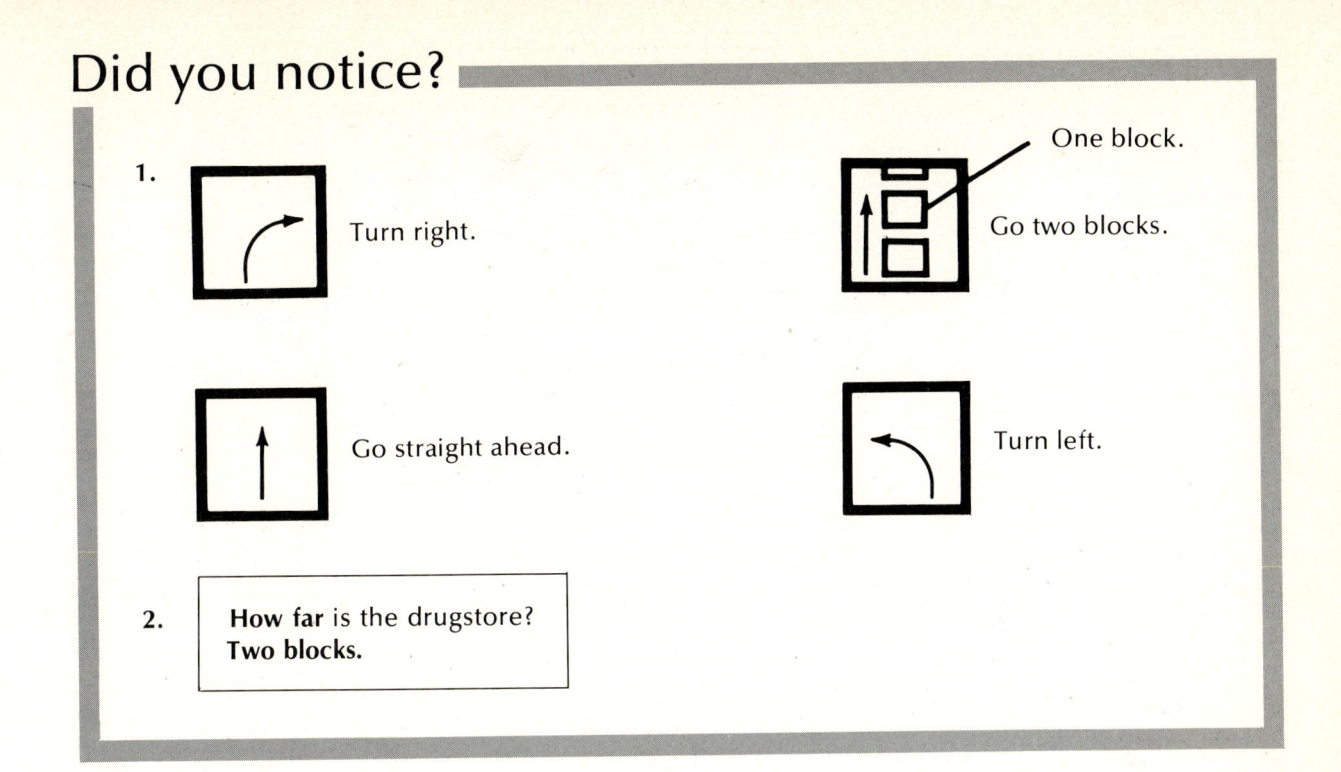

Did you notice?

1. Turn right.

   One block.
   Go two blocks.

   Go straight ahead.

   Turn left.

2. **How far** is the drugstore?
   Two blocks.

How to Say It

HOW DO WE GET TO HAMBURGER HEAVEN RESTAURANT?

3RD ST. EISENHOWER

GO ONE BLOCK TO SECOND. TURN LEFT AND GO ONE BLOCK. HAMBURGER HEAVEN'S ON THE CORNER OF SECOND AND JOHNSON.

THANKS A LOT.

Did you notice the difference?

How far is the Post Office?
   One block.
How do we get to the Post Office?
   Go one block and turn left.

Practice saying these directions.

Go one block.   Turn left.
Go straight ahead.   Turn right.

69

How about a little practice?

For two students: give directions. Use the map on page 66. You are on the corner of Johnson Road and Third Street.

1. Student 1: How do we get to Carl's Barber Shop?
   Student 2: _____

2. Student 1: How do we get to the National Bank?
   Student 2: _____

3. Student 1: How do we get to the French Bakery?
   Student 2: _____

4. Student 1: Is there a drugstore around here?
   Student 2: Yes. On Kennedy.
   Student 1: On Kennedy?
   Student 2: Yes. Go _____.

5. Student 1: Is there a beauty salon around here?
   Student 2: Yes. On Johnson.
   Student 1: Johnson?
   Student 2: Yes. Go _____.

How about a little more practice?

For two students: ask and answer questions about your city.

Student 1: Is there a _____ around here?
Student 2: _____ .

Language Game: Where Are You?

For two students: practice giving and listening to directions. Use the map on page 66.

Student 1: Give directions.
Student 2: Look at the map and listen to Student 1. Tell where you are.

1. Student 1: You're on the corner of Eisenhower Boulevard and Third Street.
   Go two blocks to First Street.
   Turn left.
   Go one block.
   Turn left.
   Go one block.
   Where are you?
   Student 2: I'm _____.

2. Student 1: You're on _____.
   Go _____.
   Turn _____.
   Go _____.
   Turn _____.
   Where are you?
   Student 2: I'm _____.

7 Citizens of the World

Read this story by yourself.
Then read it with your teacher.

Flight 18

PART ONE

Flight Attendant:	Seat 15B. On the right, sir.
Jim:	Thanks. 15B. Three . . . seven . . . ten . . . twelve . . . thirteen . . . fifteen. 15B. Hi! Are you 15A?
Abel:	Yes.
Jim:	Good. I'm 15B. My name is Jim—Jim Turner.
Abel:	Pleased to meet you. I'm Abel Lema.
Jim:	Where are you from, Africa?
Abel:	Yes.
Jim:	Where in Africa?
Abel:	East Africa, Tanzania.

Jim: Lions and tigers, huh?
Abel: No. There aren't any tigers in Africa.
Jim: No?
Abel: No, only in Asia.
Jim: Oh.
Abel: Where are you from?
Jim: Everywhere.
Abel: Excuse me. Everywhere?
Jim: My father is a businessman. His business is in Paris, in Caracas, in London, in Cairo. We live everywhere. You know.
Abel: Everywhere! You're right.

PART TWO

Kathy is a flight attendant. She's tall and pretty. She does her job and smiles. She is on her feet for hours—and smiles. It's not an easy job, but she likes it. She especially likes the New York–Bogotá run.

She sits down for a minute. Four hours to go. What, again? It's 15B. What does he want now? Another drink? She gets up and goes to Jim's seat. Yes, he wants another drink. He says he's twenty-one.

Kathy sits down again. The old couple. They're nice. They talk to everyone. She says they are retired. This is their first vacation in forty years. Good for them.

That Colombian girl in 22C. She looks so unhappy. The man in 22B is nice. It's good he speaks Spanish.

PART THREE

Jim: Do you want a drink?
Abel: No, thanks.
Jim: Sure?
Abel: Yes. Thank you. Maybe later.
Jim: Is this your first trip to New York?
Abel: Yes.
Jim: It's a great place. Business or pleasure?
Abel: School.
Jim: Oh? Where?
Abel: Columbia.
Jim: What's your field?
Abel: Engineering.
Jim: Really? My uncle is an engineer. He's in Venezuela now.
Abel: Oh? What does he do?
Jim: He builds roads, bridges—things like that.
Abel: That's what I want to do. Where do you go to school, Jim?
Jim: Princeton. In New Jersey. About an hour and a half from New York.
Abel: What year are you in?
Jim: I start in September.
Abel: What do you want to study?
Jim: I don't know. I want to have a good time: parties, girls, sports—you know.
Abel: Uh-huh.
Jim: Do you travel a lot?

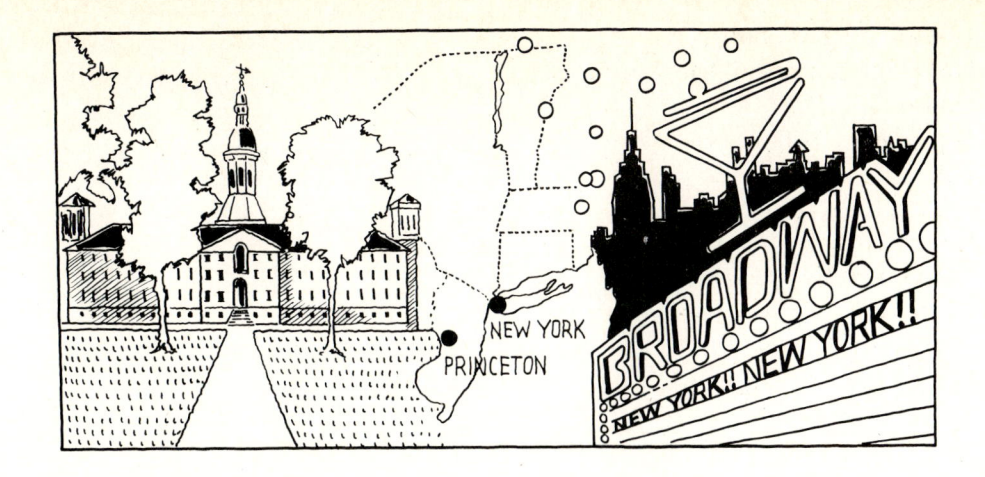

Abel: No. This is my first trip anywhere, but my uncle lives in New York.
Jim: Oh, then you have no problem. Do you like your uncle?
Abel: Of course.
Jim: Why "of course"?
Abel: Of course I like him. He's my uncle. Americans don't like their uncles?
Jim: Some uncles are okay and some aren't.
Abel: Oh.
Jim: You know, it's just like brothers and sisters. Some are great and some aren't.
Abel: Do you have any brothers and sisters?
Jim: One sister. No brothers. Wait. (He gets out his wallet.) Look, here's her picture. Isn't she pretty?
Abel: You're very . . .
Jim: Very what?
Abel: We don't talk about our sisters or say they're pretty. It's terrible.
Jim: Oh? Why?
Abel: It's not nice.
Jim: Well, it's okay in the States.
Abel: Yes?
Jim: Huh . . . and you never talk about your sisters?
Abel: Never.
Jim: Huh.

Work with the dialogue.

1. Listen to your teacher or other Americans read the dialogue in Parts One and Three. Listen to the sounds.

2. Get into groups of three, and act out the dialogue.

   Student 1: The Director
   Student 2: Jim
   Student 3: Abel

3. Get into groups of four. Play with the dialogue in Parts One and Three.

   a. Change Jim and Abel to **Mary** and **Celia**. Mary is from Boston. Celia is from São Paulo, Brazil. Mary thinks there are snakes and a jungle in São Paulo. Change other parts of the dialogue. Use your imagination. Act out your new dialogue for the class.

b. Change Jim and Abel to **Brian,** a young man from Texas, and **Emilia,** a young lady from Colombia. Brian likes Emilia. Change the dialogue as much as you want. Have fun. Act out the dialogue for the class.

Use the English you know—role-play.

Get into groups of five.

Situation 1: You're in English class on the first day.

    Student 1: A Student
    Student 2: The Teacher
    Teacher: Hello, I'm your teacher, _____.
                                                    (name)
    Student: Pleased to meet you, _____.

Continue the conversation.

Situation 2: You're on a plane.

    Student 1: A Passenger
    Student 2: A Passenger
    Student 1 begins, "Is this your first trip to _____?"

Continue the conversation. Look at Part Three for ideas.

Situation 3: You're on a plane.

    Student 1: A Passenger
    Student 2: A Passenger
    Student 1 begins the conversation, "Do you travel a lot?"

Continue the conversation.

    a. Talk about where you go.
    b. Talk about how often you take trips.
    c. Ask, "Do you like to travel?"

Use the English you know—be yourself.

Get into groups of four. Choose two students to be the actors.

Situation 1: You're at a Christmas party for ESL students.

    Student 1: "Hi, I'm _____."
    Student 2: "Pleased to meet you."

Continue the conversation. Tell your name and talk about where you and the other person are from. Use the dialogue as a guide.

Situation 2: You are passengers on a plane.

    A student begins, "What's your field?" or "What do you do?"

Look at Part Three for ideas. Continue the conversation. Talk about your fields of study or your jobs.

Situation 3: You're in a restaurant with a new friend.

    Student 1:   "Do you come from a large family?"
    Student 2:   _____

Continue the conversation. Talk about your families (sisters, brothers, aunts, uncles, cousins). Talk about where they live. Talk about what they do.

Extend your vocabulary.

It's okay to use your dictionary.

1. In a group of four students, describe a flight attendant you have seen. Look at Part Two for ideas. Help your fellow students with vocabulary words or other problems. Ask one student to write it all down. Give it to your teacher.

2. Be yourself and describe what you do every day. Write it down. Give it to your teacher.

8 What Are You Doing After Class?

How to Say It

She's carrying her bags.

CARRY her bags

He's watching a movie.

WATCH a movie

Did you notice?

PRESENT PROGRESSIVE TENSE

IS	BASE FORM + ING
is	carrying
is	watching

Practice saying these sentences.

>She's carrying her bags.
>He's watching a movie.

How to Say It

GET ON a plane

TALK

Practice saying these sentences.

>They're getting on a plane.
>They're talking.

Study this grammar.

SUBJECT	AM/IS/ARE	BASE FORM + ING	
She / He	is	carrying	her bags.
She's			
He's		watching	a movie.
They	are	talking.	
They're			

How about a little practice?

Make statements about what is happening in these pictures. (Use Visual Aids #s 11–19.)

CARRY her bags

TAKE OUT her ticket

GET ON the plane

SIT

TALK

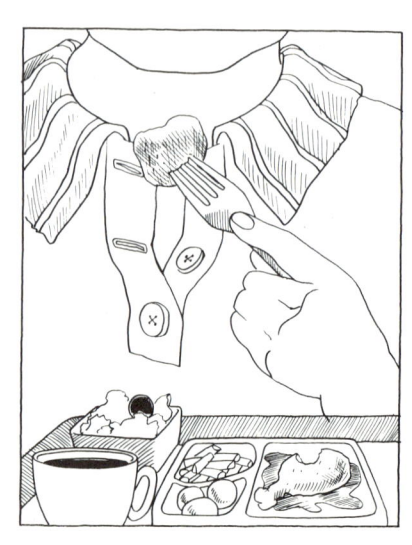

EAT

READ a magazine   WATCH a movie   SLEEP

How to Say It

WHAT'S HE DOING?
HE'S WORKING, BUT HE WANTS TO GO TO SLEEP.

WORK/GO to sleep

WHAT'S HE DOING?
HE'S TAKING A BUS, BUT HE WANTS TO TAKE A TAXI.

TAKE a bus/TAKE a taxi

Did you notice?

QUESTION	What	is	he		doing?
STATEMENT			He	is	working.

Practice saying these sentences.

What's he doing?
He's working.
He wants to go to sleep.

He's taking a bus.
He wants to take a taxi.

79

How about a little practice?

For two students: ask and answer questions about what is happening in the pictures below. (Use Visual Aids #s 20–25).

    Student 1:   What _____ doing?
    Student 2:   _____ , but _____ .

WORK/
WATCH TV

SIT in school/
PLAY baseball

WASH the floor/
GO shopping

TAKE a bus/
TAKE a taxi

COOK/
GO to a movie

WORK/
GO to sleep.

80

Read this dialogue with your teacher.

(José is calling Francesca.)

Francesca: Hello.
José: Hello, Francesca?
Francesca: Yes.
José: This is José. From your English class.
Francesca: Hi, José.
José: What are you doing?
Francesca: Watching TV.
José: A good show?
Francesca: So-so. So, what's happening?
José: **What are you doing after class?**
Francesca: After class?
José: Yeah. Wednesday. After class.
Francesca: I don't know.
José: **Would you like to go out for coffee?**
Francesca: All right.
José: So how are you?
Francesca: Fine, and you?
José: Fine. Ah . . . well listen. See you Wednesday.
Francesca: Right.
José: Okay. Good. See you then. Bye.
Francesca: (Francesca is smiling.) Bye-bye.

Did you notice?

1.

NOW	FUTURE
What are you doing?	What are you doing after class?

2.

INVITING		
WOULD YOU LIKE TO	BASE FORM	
Would you like to	go out	for coffee?

Study this vocabulary.

| Sunday | Monday | Tuesday | Wednesday | Thursday | Friday | Saturday |

Practice saying these sentences.

Where are you going Sunday?
To church.
Where are you going Tuesday evening?
To school.

Where are you going after class?
Home.

Study this grammar.

go to	the the the the the	bank movies post office supermarket library
	a a	restaurant coffee shop
		school church work
go		home

How about a little practice?

Example:

> Where are you going Saturday evening?
> To my friend's house, and then we're going to the movies.

For two students: ask and answer. Use different days of the week.

> Student 1: Where are you going _____ ?
> Student 2: _____

How to Say It

[Comic panel 1: "FUSAKO, WOULD YOU LIKE TO GO OUT FOR COFFEE?" "SURE. WHEN?"]

[Comic panel 2: "HOW ABOUT AFTER CLASS?" "FINE. SEE YOU THEN."]

Study these language functions.

INVITING

	VERY FORMAL → → → →		INFORMAL
INVITING	Would you like to join me for coffee?	Would you like to go out for coffee?	Want to go out for coffee?
ACCEPTING INVITATIONS	Certainly. I'd like to very much.	Thank you. That would be nice.	Sure. (or) Okay.
ASKING FOR INFORMATION	When would you like to go?	When do you want to go?	When?
INVITING	Would after class be a good time?	Would after class be all right?	How about after class?
ACCEPTING AN INVITATION	That would be fine.	Fine.	Good. (or) Okay.
CONFIRMING AN INVITATION	So, we'll meet after class.	See you then.	See you.

Did you notice?

It is possible to change from formal to informal in the middle of a conversation.

Practice saying these sentences.

Would you like to go out for coffee?
Sure. When?
How about after class?
See you then.
Fine.

How to Say It

> WOULD YOU LIKE TO GO TO A MOVIE?
> WHEN?
> ON SATURDAY?

> OH, I'M SORRY. I CAN'T.
> MAYBE SOME OTHER TIME.

Study these language functions.

	VERY FORMAL → → → →		INFORMAL
DECLINING AN INVITATION	I'm very sorry, but I'm not able to come.	I'm sorry. I can't make it.	Sorry. I can't.

Practice saying these sentences.

Would you like to go to a movie?
I'm sorry. I can't.

How about a little practice?

For two students: practice inviting and saying "yes" or "no."
Use this vocabulary:

go to a movie
come to dinner
go to a party
go shopping
go dancing

>> WOULD YOU LIKE TO GO TO A MOVIE?
>> SURE.

Example:

Student 1: Would you _____ ?
Student 2: _____

Read this dialogue with your teacher.

(On the phone)

Doctor: **How are you, Mrs. Karkosza?**
Sophie: **Not so good.**
Doctor: **What's the matter?**
Sophie: **I can't sleep.**
Doctor: **Hmmm.**

Sophie: I have a very bad backache.
Doctor: **Can** you come to the office?
Sophie: I think so.
Doctor: Come right now.
Sophie: Thank you, Doctor.

Did you notice?

1.

			CAN (ABILITY)		
			MODAL AUXILIARY	BASE FORM	
NEGATIVE STATEMENT		I	can't	sleep.	
QUESTION	Can	you		come	to the office?

2.

can	not
can't	

←a contraction

85

Practice saying these sentences.

How are you?
Not so good.
What's the matter?
I can't sleep.
I have a backache.
Can you come to the office?

Study this vocabulary.

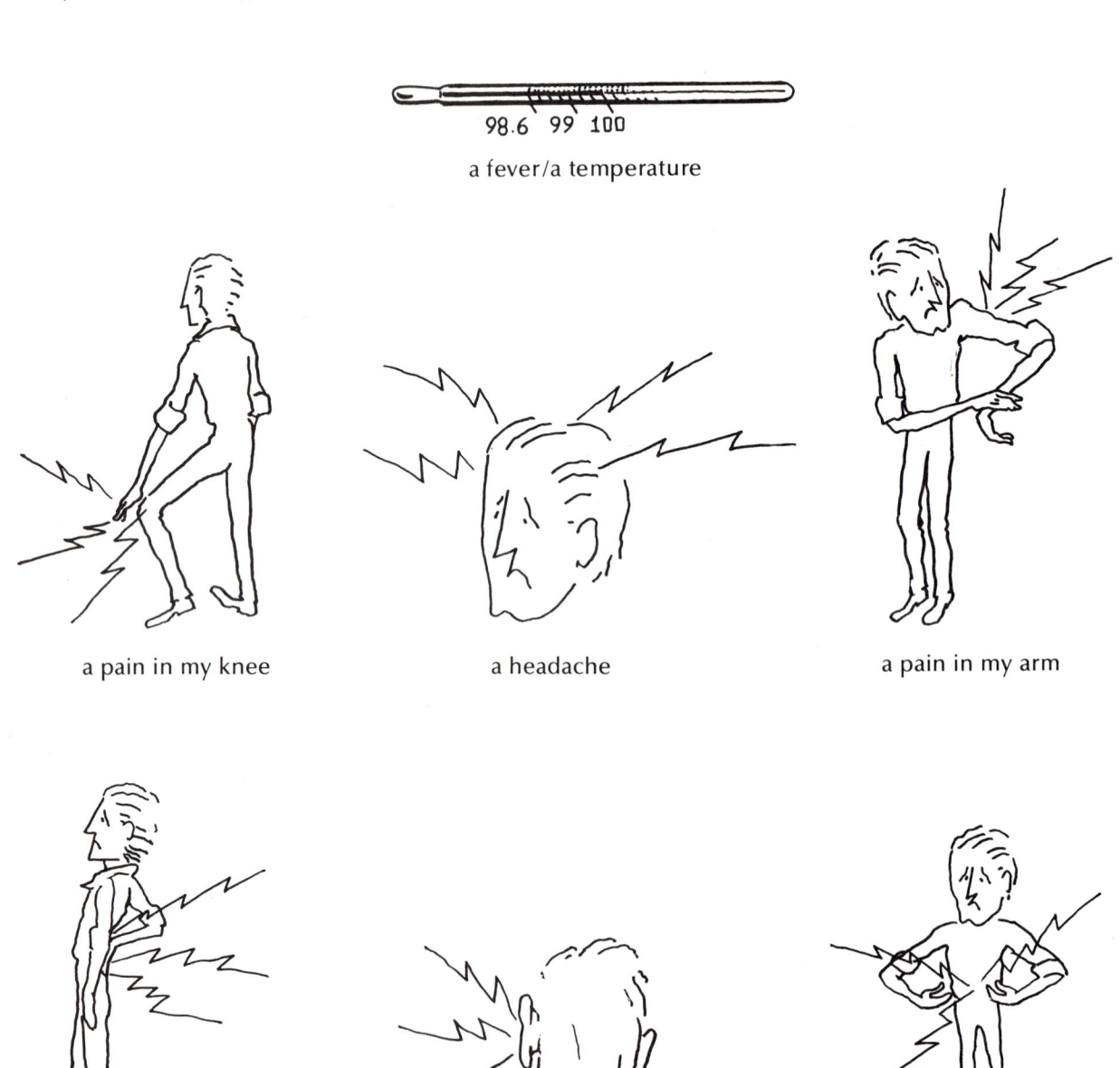

a fever/a temperature

a pain in my knee

a headache

a pain in my arm

a backache

an earache

a stomachache

Language Game: Help! I'm Dying.

Example:

> OOOH!
> WHAT'S THE MATTER?
> OW!
> DO YOU HAVE A STOMACHACHE?
> OOOH! YES.
> OH, I'M SORRY.

For two students:

    Student 1:   Pretend you are sick. Use your imagination.
    Student 2:   Find out what the matter is. Express sympathy.

Study these language functions.

EXPRESSING SYMPATHY

VERY FORMAL →	→ → → →	INFORMAL
I'm very sorry to hear that (*person*) is ill.	I'm sorry to hear (*person*) is sick.	Sorry to hear that.
That's a shame.	I'm sorry.	Sorry.
Please give (*person*) my best regards.	Tell (*person*) I'm thinking about (*him* or *her*).	Tell (*person*) I'm thinking about (*person*).

How to Say It

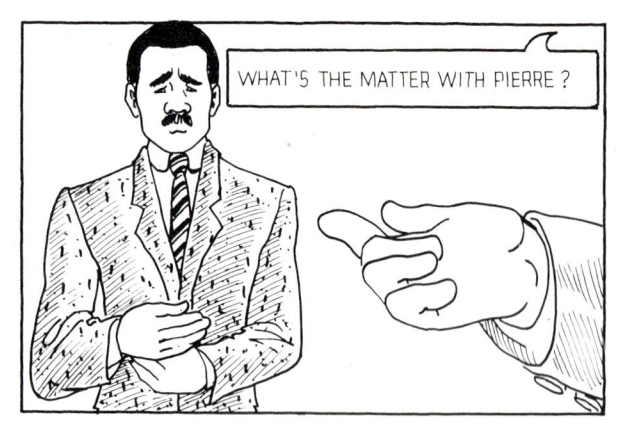

> WHAT'S THE MATTER WITH PIERRE?
>
> HE HAS A STOMACHACHE AND CAN'T EAT.
>
> I'M SORRY TO HEAR THAT. TELL HIM I'M THINKING ABOUT HIM.

Practice saying these sentences.

What's the matter with Pierre?
He has a stomachache and can't eat.
I'm sorry to hear that.
Tell him I'm thinking about him.

For two students: ask and answer questions about different problems.

Practice expressing sympathy.

1.

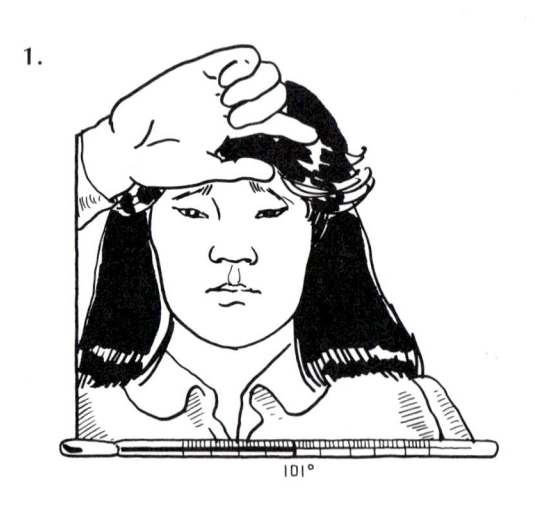

Fusako/go to school

Student 1: What's the matter with _____?
Student 2: _____ has _____ and can't _____.
Student 1: I'm sorry to hear that. Tell _____ I'm thinking about _____.

2.

Karim/study

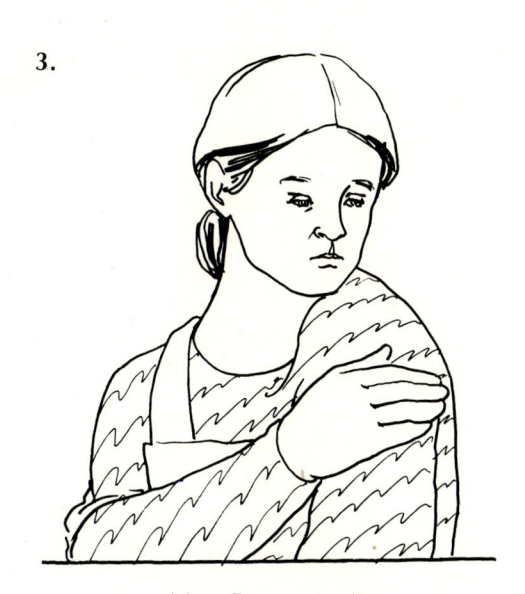

3.

Mrs. Popov/write

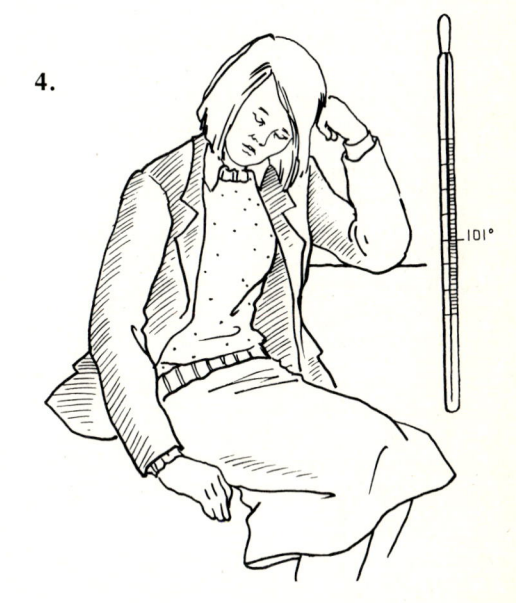

4.

Susan Gutierrez/teach

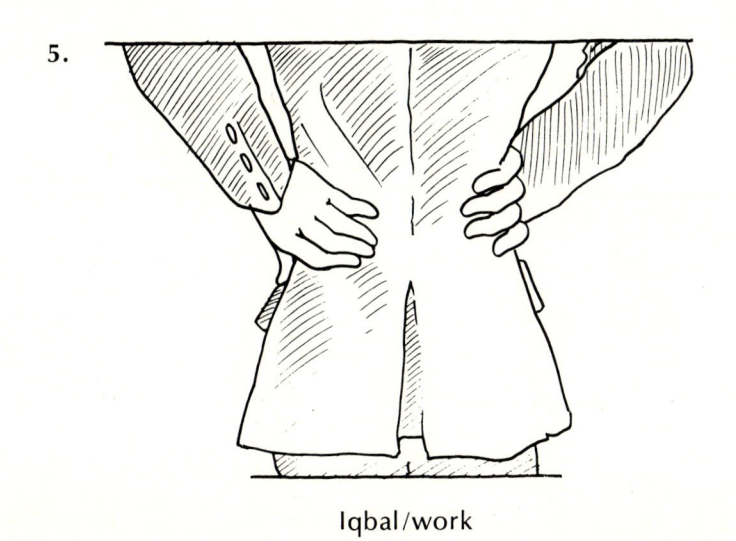

5.

Iqbal/work

89

How to Say It

Practice saying these sentences.

    I can speak English.
    /kIn/
    I can't read Arabic.
    /kænt/

How about a little practice?

Make statements about what you can and can't do.

    I can/can't speak _____ .
    I can/can't read _____ .
    I can/can't write _____ .
    I can/can't understand _____ .

How about a little more practice?

Look at Visual Aids #26. Show the class something you can do. Make a statement.

Example:

9 Where Were You When I Called?

How to Say It

Panel 1:
— CAN YOU SPEAK FRENCH?
— YES. PRETTY WELL.

Panel 2:
— WHERE DID YOU LEARN?
— IN SCHOOL.

Panel 3:
— CAN YOU DRIVE?
— SURE.

Panel 4:
— WHERE DID YOU LEARN?
— FROM MY FATHER.

Did you notice?

1.

		AUXILIARY VERB	SUBJECT	MAIN VERB (BASE FORM)
PAST TENSE	Where	did	you	learn?
PRESENT TENSE	Where	do	you	live?

2.

LEARN IN + PLACE
I learned French **in** Canada.

LEARN FROM + PERSON
I learned Spanish **from** my grandmother.

Practice saying this sentence.

Where did you learn?

For two students: ask and answer.

Use these verbs.

drive   cook
speak   dance
sew

Student 1: Can you _____?
Student 2: _____
Student 1: Where did you learn?
Student 2: _____

92

How to Say It

> CAN YOU REMEMBER PHONE NUMBERS?
> SURE.

> HOW DO YOU DO IT?
> I DON'T KNOW. I JUST CAN.

> CAN YOU REMEMBER NUMBERS?
> I CAN'T. CAN YOU?

> SOMETIMES.

Practice saying these sentences.

Can you remember numbers?
Sometimes.

How do you do it?
I don't know. I just can.

For two students: ask and answer.

Use these words.

phone numbers	faces
names	addresses
dates	directions

Student 1: Can you remember _____?
Student 2: _____

How to Say It

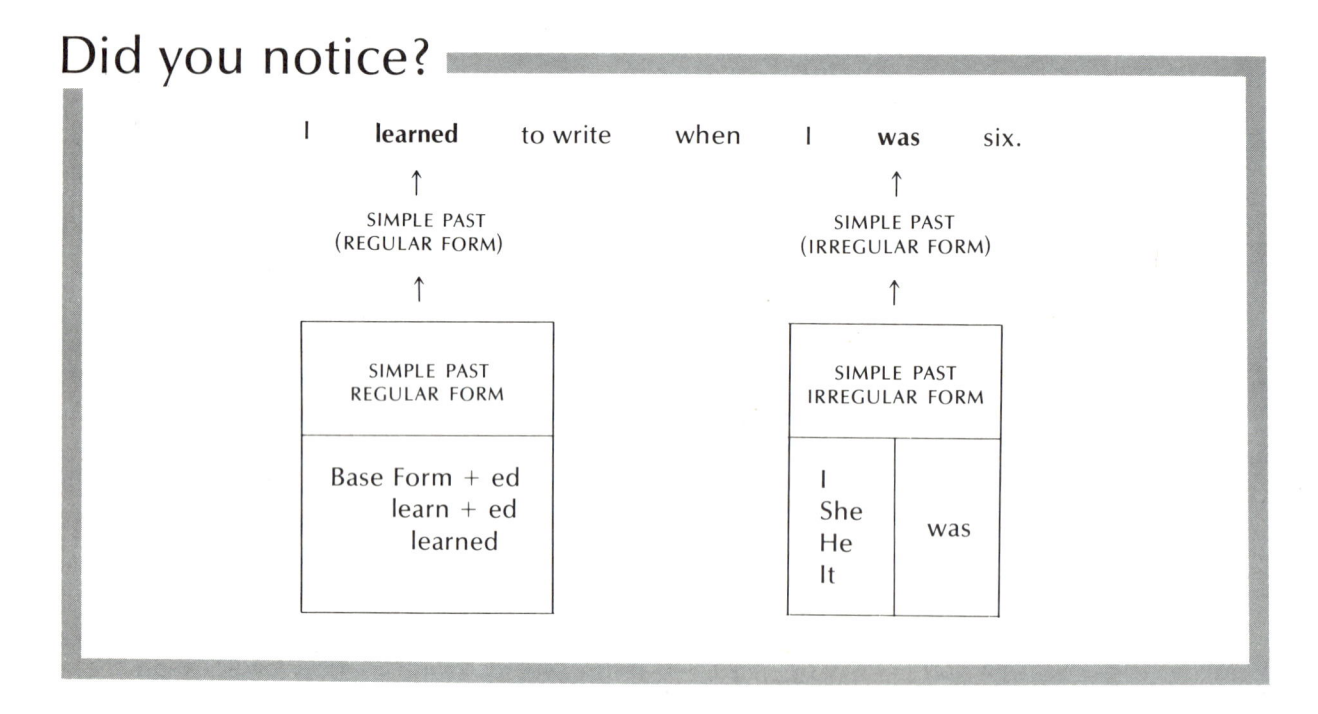

[Comic: Two men talking. One says "I LEARNED TO TALK WHEN I WAS 2." The other says "I LEARNED TO DRIVE WHEN I WAS 18."]

Did you notice?

I **learned** to write when I **was** six.

↑ SIMPLE PAST (REGULAR FORM)   ↑ SIMPLE PAST (IRREGULAR FORM)

SIMPLE PAST REGULAR FORM
Base Form + ed
learn + ed
learned

SIMPLE PAST IRREGULAR FORM
I, She, He, It — was

Practice saying these sentences.

I learned to drive when I was 18.
I learned to talk when I was 2.

How about a little practice?

Make five statements. Use these words.

talk	walk	speak English
cook	drive	read
write	dance	swim

I learned to _____ when I was _____.

94

Read these two dialogues with your teacher.

Dialogue One

    Milton Chase: What do you do?
    Nikolai Popov: I'm not working now. I'm learning English.
    Milton Chase: Oh. Did you work in your country?
    Nikolai Popov: I was a computer programmer.
    Milton Chase: What do you want to do when you finish studying?
    Nikolai Popov: I want to be a computer programmer again.

Dialogue Two

    Milton Chase: What do you do?
    José Dorado: I'm studying to be an electrical technician.
    Milton Chase: Did you work in your country?
    José Dorado: Yes. I was a mechanic.
    Milton Chase: So now you want to be an electrical technician?
    José Dorado: Uh-uh.

Practice saying these sentences.

    What do you do?
    What did you do in your country?
    What do you want to be?

For two students: ask and answer.

    Student 1:   What do you do?
    Student 2:   _____
    Student 1:   What did you do in your country?
    Student 2:   _____
    Student 1:   What do you want to be?
    Student 2:   _____

How to Say It

Practice saying these sentences.

What time is it?
Three o'clock.

For two students: ask and answer.

Student 1: What time is it?
Student 2: _____

1. 
2. 
3. 
4. 
5. 
6.

Study these phrases.

eleven o'clock

eleven-o-five
five after eleven

eleven fifteen
a quarter after eleven

eleven thirty
half past eleven

eleven forty-five
a quarter to twelve

eleven fifty
ten to twelve

96

Practice saying these phrases.

eleven-o-five
five after eleven
a quarter after eleven
half past eleven
a quarter to twelve
ten to twelve

How about a little practice?

Practice saying these times.

1. 

2. 9:35

3. 

4. 7:45

5. 

6. 8:00

Study this vocabulary.

12:00
noon

12:00
midnight

Read this story with your teacher.

Monday

    Steve Kern: Where were you at noon yesterday?
    Carmen Lopez: At noon? At work. Why?
    Steve Kern: Oh . . . just asking.

Tuesday

    Steve Kern: Where were you last night at seven?
    Carmen Lopez: At home.
    Steve Kern: I called, but there was no answer.
    Carmen Lopez: I was home.

Wednesday

    Steve Kern: Where were you . . . ?
    Carmen Lopez: Hold it! Wait a minute.
    Steve Kern: What?
    Carmen Lopez: "Where were you? Where were you? Where were you?" You're driving me crazy.
    Steve Kern: But, Carmen. . .
    Carmen Lopez: You're not my father, Steve. And you're certainly not my husband.
    Steve Kern: Okay. Okay. I'm sorry.

Study this grammar.

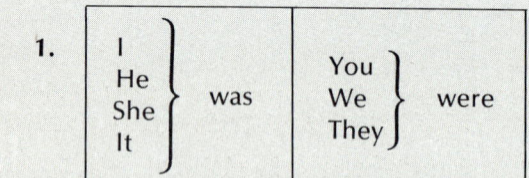

1. | I / He / She / It | was | You / We / They | were |

2. AT + CLOCK TIME
    at   noon
    at   7:00

3. at home
   at school
   at work
   at the movies
   at the bank
   at my friend's house
   in a restaurant
   in a store
   in my apartment
   in my car
   on a plane
   on a bus

Practice saying these sentences.

    Where were you last night at seven?
    Where were you yesterday at noon?

For two students: ask and answer.

    Student 1:   Where were you at _____ ?
                                      (time)
    Student 2:   _____

Study this grammar.

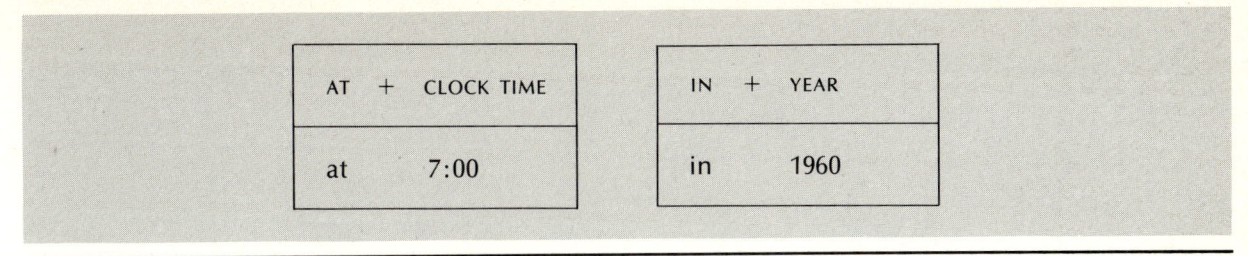

AT	+	CLOCK TIME
at		7:00

IN	+	YEAR
in		1960

Language Game: Where and When

Example:

> WHERE WERE YOU IN 1960?
>
> I WAS IN SCHOOL IN ANN ARBOR, MICHIGAN.
>
> AND WHERE WERE YOU IN 1943?
>
> MILTON! I WASN'T BORN YET! WHERE WERE YOU?
>
> I WAS IN THE ARMY IN ENGLAND.

For two students: ask and answer.

    Student 1: Where were you in _____?
    Student 2: _____

**Read this story by yourself.
Then read it with your teacher.**

PART FOUR

      (Jay and Matilde, seats 22B and 22C, are speaking in Spanish. This is a translation.)

Jay: Excuse me. Are you all right? I . . .
Matilde: I'm sorry. Really. (She cries again.) I'm just . . .
Jay: It's hard to leave home. I know. But the U.S. isn't so bad.
Matilde: I know. I'm just . . . I don't know. I'm sad. (She cries a little more.) Sad and a little nervous.
Jay: It's natural. But don't be afraid. Don't worry.
Matilde: I know you're right. I can't help it.
Jay: Where are you from?
Matilde: Bogotá. And you?
Jay: New York.
Matilde: You're a Colombian, aren't you?
Jay: I was born in Colombia. I'm an American citizen now. Oh, excuse me. My name is Jay Gutierrez.
Matilde: Jay?
Jay: My real name is Julio. Americans call me Jay.
Matilde: Oh . . . My name is Matilde Rojas.
Jay: Pleased to meet you.
Matilde: (She smiles.) Do you really like it?
Jay: The U.S.? Yes. Well, yes and no. You know.
Matilde: Is it true? Is everybody rich?
Jay: No. Some are, of course. You can see them on Fifth Avenue. Most of us work hard for our money.
Matilde: Is New York very exciting? My mother and father live there.
Jay: Where do they live?
Matilde: Queens.
Jay: Really? I live there, too. There are thousands of Colombians in Queens.
Matilde: Thousands?

Jay: Yes, and thousands of Greeks, Italians, Russians, Chinese, Haitians, Ecuadorians, Dominicans—thousands of people of every nationality.
Matilde: That's very exciting. And thousands of Colombians, you say. That's good. My English isn't very good.
Jay: Don't worry. There are millions of Latin Americans in New York. In fact, you don't have to speak any English.
Matilde: I can't stay home, you know. I need to get a job and help my family. Can I get a job right away?
Jay: You can get a job in a factory. Then you can study English at night.
Matilde: Do you think so?
Jay: Sure. My wife teaches English.
Matilde: In New York?
Jay: Yes.
Matilde: She's American?
Jay: Yes.
Matilde: Are schools expensive?
Jay: Some are. But some are free.
Matilde: Where does your wife work? Can you give me the address?
Jay: Sure. (He writes the address on a card.)
Matilde: (She starts to cry again.)
Jay: What's the matter?
Matilde: Nothing. I'm sorry. I miss Colombia.
Jay: Already?
Matilde: It's silly. I know.

PART FIVE

(Alice and George Hess, seats 22E and 22F, are talking.)

Alice: I hope the house is all right.
George: It's good to go home.
Alice: A wonderful vacation.
George: Except for that stomach trouble in Cuzco.
Alice: Oh, George. What's an upset stomach? Macchu Picchu was wonderful. Wonderful. I want to go back.
George: Back? What about Hawaii? We can sit on the beach and look at the water.
Alice: You go to Hawaii. You sit all day. I can still walk and see things.
George: (George laughs.) Alice. You're wonderful. Where do you want to go next year? Nepal, West Africa, China? We can go anywhere, you and I.
Alice: Yes, we can, dear. But it is good to go home.
George: I hope they're waiting for us at the airport.
Alice: They always are.
George: I miss the grandchildren.
Alice: I miss them, too. You know, little Georgie is just like you—in every way. He looks like you, he talks like you, he walks like you.
George: I love that kid.
Alice: You're a good grandfather.
George: And you're a good grandmother, dear.
Alice: Mmmm.
George: Next year—Africa. What do you say?
Alice: Africa? Why not?

George: Do you see that girl across the aisle? Poor girl. She cries every five minutes. I think she's leaving home for good.
Alice: Yes. It's hard to leave your country and friends.
George: Hard at any age.
Alice: What time is it, dear?
George: We have another three hours to go. How about a drink?
Alice: Good idea. Planes are wonderful but boring.
George: (To the flight attendant) Two champagnes, please. (To Alice) Do you remember our honeymoon?
Alice: That was a different world. 1938. Before the War.
George: Before the store, too.
Alice: And the kids.
George: Yes.
Alice: Wasn't it romantic? The *Queen Mary* was a beautiful ship, remember?
George: Remember the dining room?
Alice: And I remember how handsome you were in your new dinner jacket. Every minute was exciting.
Kathy: (To George) Your drinks, sir.
George: Thank you. (To Alice) To the *Queen Mary*.
Alice: To the *Queen Mary*.

PART SIX

(Jay is showing Matilde the pictures in his wallet.)

Jay: And this one is Johnny. He's three and a half.
Matilde: And this one?
Jay: That's Raul. We call him Ralph. He's seven. He's my boy. He looks like my wife.
Matilde: Yes. He looks like an American.
Jay: And this is my wife, Susan. She has dirt on her face. She's working in the garden.
Matilde: Oh, how pretty.
Jay: She is. And this is a picture of our house.
Matilde: It's beautiful.
Jay: It's small, but we like it.
Matilde: Where is it?
Jay: Whitestone. You and your parents have to visit us.
Matilde: I'd like to.
Jay: And what about you?
Matilde: I'm eighteen years old. I was born in Bogotá. Uh . . . that's it.
Jay: Why are you leaving Colombia?
Matilde: My parents want me to.
Jay: And you don't want to.
Matilde: I want to go home. (She cries.) I don't want to leave Colombia.
Jay: Do you have a boyfriend?
Matilde: Yes.
Jay: Ah . . . well.
Matilde: I don't know anybody in New York. Only my parents.
Jay: Don't you have any brothers or sisters?
Matilde: No. I have cousins in Colombia. That's all.
Jay: It's lonely for a while, but then . . . life goes on.
Matilde: I guess so.

Work with the dialogue.

1. Listen to your teacher or other Americans read the dialogues. Listen to the sounds.

2. Get into groups of three. Act out the dialogues in Parts Four, Five, and Six for the class.

   Part Four
   Student 1:   The Director   Student 2:   Jay   Student 3:   Matilde

   Part Five
   Student 1:   Alice   Student 2:   The Director   Student 3:   George

   Part Six
   Student 1:   Jay   Student 2:   Matilde   Student 3:   The Director

3. Get into groups of three. Play with the dialogue. Have one person be the director.

   In Part Five, Alice and George are very positive. Change George to a very negative person. Start the dialogue this way:

   Alice: I hope the house is all right.
   George: It probably burned down.
   Alice: Oh, George. It was a wonderful vacation.
   George: It was terrible. I got sick in Cuzco.

   Continue the dialogue. Use your imagination. Act out the new dialogue for the class.

Use the English you know—role-play.

Get into groups of five. Choose two students to be the actors.

Situation 1: You're on a plane.

   Student 1:   Are you going to Miami?
   Student 2:   No, I'm going to Montreal, Canada.
   Student 1:   But this plane is going to Florida. South.
   Student 2:   No, it isn't.

Continue the conversation. Have fun!

103

Situation 2: You're on a plane.

 Student 1: Do you want a magazine?
 Student 2: No, thanks. I'd like to sleep.
 Student 1: You can't!
 Student 2: What?
 Student 1: I want you to look at twenty pictures of my three ugly children and one hundred pictures of my vacation.

Continue the conversation. Have fun!

Use the English you know—be yourself.

Situation 1: You're on a plane.

Student 1: A person not from the United States.
Student 2: A person from the United States.

 Student 1: Are you going to _____?
           (a city)
 Student 2: Yes. And you?
 Student 1: Yes. This is my first trip to the United States.
 Student 2: Welcome. I live in _____.
          (a city)

Continue the conversation. Ask about the city. Ask about Americans.

Situation 2: You're on a plane.

Student 1: Your first trip to the United States.
Student 2: You live in the United States.

 Student 1: Do you like the United States?
 Student 2: Yes. Yes and no, you know.

Continue the conversation. Student 1, ask questions. Student 2, tell the good points and bad points of life in the United States.

Extend your vocabulary.

In groups of four to six, plan a vacation together. It's okay to use your dictionary.

 Student 1: Where do you want to go next year?
 Student 2: I don't know. Where do you want to go?
 Student 3: What about Hawaii?
 Student 4: No. It's too expensive. What about _____?

Continue the conversation. Discuss two or three different places. Finally, decide where you want to go and how long you want to stay there.

10 She Turned on the TV and Fell Asleep

Read these paragraphs with your teacher.

José **called** Pierre yesterday because he **wanted** to use Pierre's stereo. He **talked** to Pierre for a few minutes and then **asked** him, "Can I borrow your stereo? I'm giving a party on Saturday."
Pierre **answered,** "Sorry, José. I'm giving one on Saturday, too."

Pronunciation practice.

called	talked	wanted
/d/	/t/	/Id/
answered	asked	
/d/	/t/	

Did you notice?

The **regular simple past tense** has three different pronunciations. Compare these with the pronunciations of the plural on page 22.

Practice saying these words.

/d/	/t/	/Id/
learned	talked	needed
played	walked	wanted
examined	kissed	tasted
listened	fixed	waited
ordered	parked	
turned	looked	
called	missed	
arrived	worked	
	asked	
	cooked	

105

How to Say It

(Look at Visual Aids #s 27–31.)

(After school yesterday) GO home

(and) EAT dinner.

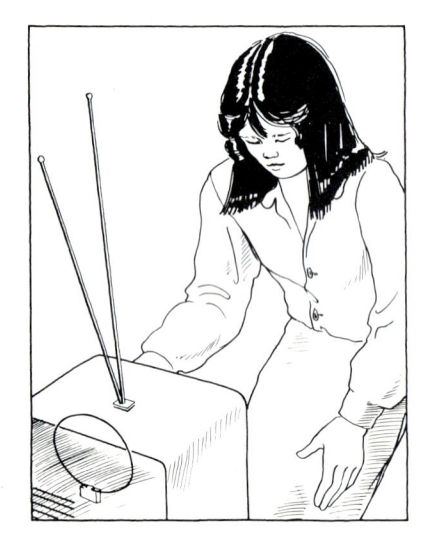

(Then) TURN ON TV

(and) WATCH the news.

(But) FALL ASLEEP five minutes later.

New irregular verbs:

BASE FORM	IRREGULAR PAST TENSE
go	went
eat	ate
fall asleep	fell asleep

Milton: Fusako looks very tired.
Francesca: She is. After school yesterday, she **went** home and **ate** dinner. Then she **turned on** the TV and **watched** the news. But she **fell asleep** five minutes later.

Practice saying these sentences.

She went home.   She ate dinner.
She turned on the TV.   She watched the news.
       /d/   /t/

How about a little practice?

1. These drawings illustrate Iqbal's visit to a new restaurant. Look at them (or at Visual Aids #s 32–36).

GO to a new restaurant.    ORDER a salad,    (and) TASTE it.

LIKE it a lot,    (so) ASK FOR three more.

For two students: ask and tell about Iqbal's visit to the new restaurant.

   Student 1:   Did Iqbal like the new restaurant?
   Student 2:   Did he like it? Let me tell you. _____

107

2. These drawings show what happened to Wen Yu this morning. Look at them (or at Visual Aids #s 37–40).

LEAVE the house at 8:00.

RUN to the bus stop,

(but) MISS the bus.

GET to work ten minutes late.

For two students: ask and tell about Wen Yu's morning.

New irregular verbs:

BASE FORM	IRREGULAR PAST TENSE
leave	left
run	ran

Student 1: What happened to Wen Yu?
Student 2: _____

3. These drawings show why Sophie missed class. Look at them (or at Visual Aids #s 41–48).

FEEL sick (so)

CALL the doctor.

TELL her, "Come to the office."

TAKE a taxi to his office.

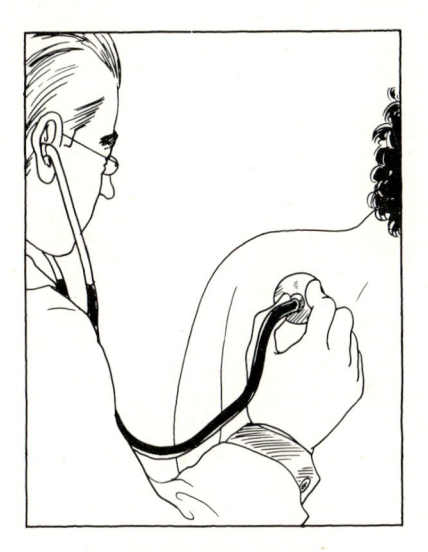

EXAMINE her

(and) TELL her, "_____."

(So) GO home,

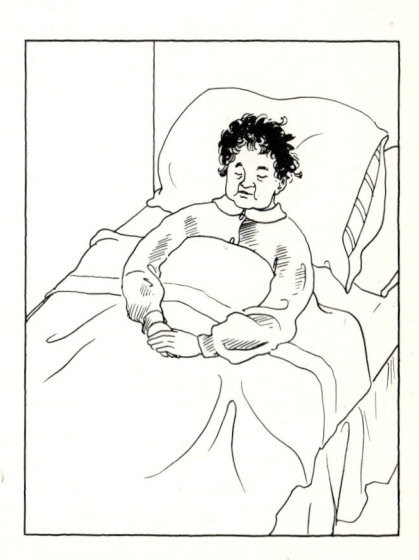

(and) GO to bed.

109

For two students: ask about and tell why Sophie missed class.

New irregular verbs:

BASE FORM	IRREGULAR PAST TENSE
feel	felt
take	took

Student 1: Where's Sophie? Why isn't she in class?
Student 2: _____

4. These drawings illustrate Mr. Kim's trip. Look at them (or at Visual Aids #s 49–57).

DRIVE to the airport (and) PARK the car. WALK to the terminal

(and) GO IN. GIVE the clerk his ticket (and) SAY, "_____."

110

TELL him, "_____." (So) BUY a newspaper (and) GO to the bar.

For two students: role-play. Student 1, take the part of Mrs. Kim. Student 2, take the part of Mr. Kim. Ask and tell about Mr. Kim's trip.

New irregular verbs:

BASE FORM	IRREGULAR PAST TENSE
drive	drove
give	gave
say	said
tell	told

Student 1: Darling! How was your trip?
Student 2: _____

How about a little more practice?

Get into groups of three. Tell your classmates about a time you

fell asleep called the doctor
had a delicious dinner kissed a friend
were late fixed something
were sick
took a trip
waited for someone

111

How to Say It

(She went to the supermarket to get some milk.)

Why did she go to the supermarket?

(She went to the store to buy a dress.)

Why did she go shopping?

Did you notice?

1.

SIMPLE PAST	Why	did	she	go shopping?
SIMPLE PRESENT		does		

2.

TO	VERB	NOUN PHRASE
to	get buy	some milk a dress

Practice saying these sentences.

She went to get some milk.
She went to buy a dress.

Language Game: Guess Why She Did That

Example:

> WHY DID MRS. POPOV GO TO THE BANK?

> MAYBE SHE WENT THERE TO GET SOME MONEY.
> MAYBE SHE WENT THERE TO GET A MONEY ORDER.
> MAYBE SHE WENT TO BUY TRAVELERS' CHECKS.

For four students: ask and answer questions about Mrs. Popov. Use these words.

drugstore
supermarket
police station
doctor's office
library
department store

Student 1: Why did Mrs. Popov go to the _____?
Student 2: Maybe she _____.
Student 3: Maybe she _____.
Student 4: Maybe she _____.

How about a little practice?

For two students: ask and answer questions about where you went this weekend.

Student 1: Where did you go this weekend?
Student 2: _____
Student 1: Why did you go there?
Student 2: _____

**Read this story by yourself.
Then read it with your teacher.**

Flight 18

PART SEVEN

Abel: Excuse me, Jim. (Abel gets up and stands in the aisle.) Uh . . . Do you know where . . . ?
Jim: They're in the back.
Abel: (Abel smiles.) Thank you. (Abel walks to the back of the plane. George and Jay are standing there.)
George: (To Abel) They're all occupied. Join the line.
Abel: Oh.
Jay: (To Abel) Hi.
Abel: Hi. (Abel smiles.)
George: (To Abel) Did you visit South America?
Abel: Yes. Colombia. My brother is studying agriculture there.
George: Really?
Jay: Is he interested in coffee growing?
Abel: Yes. We grow a lot of coffee in my country.
George: Where are you from?
Abel: East Africa. Tanzania.
Jay: Are you studying agriculture, too?
Abel: No. Engineering.
George: Where?
Abel: At Columbia University.
George: Good Luck!
Jay: Have you ever been to the States before?
Abel: No. It's my first time. . . . Is New York really dangerous, the way people say?
Jay: Parts of it are, parts of it aren't. But it's a great place. It really is.
George: I always wanted to go to Africa. Well, maybe next year. . . . (Someone comes out of the lavatory.) Finally. Nice talking to you.
Abel: Nice talking to you, sir.
George: Oh, you don't have to call me "sir." It makes me feel old.

PART EIGHT

(George goes back to his seat.)

Alice: You're back!
George: There was a line.
Alice: (Looking at the back of the plane) Yes. I see.

(Abel is walking down the aisle to his seat. He smiles at George.)

Alice: That young man has a nice smile.
George: Yes. I talked to him. He's from East Africa.
Alice: Oh, yes?
George: He's studying in the States. (George, looking around) How's the Colombian girl? Still crying?
Alice: Off and on. But the man next to her is cheering her up.
George: That's good. (George yawns.) I'm tired.
Alice: Rest. We have a couple of hours to go.
George: I can't sleep on planes.
Alice: Try. Put your head back, and close your eyes.
George: Two hours to go. The meal was terrible, wasn't it? Everything tasted like plastic.
Alice: Stop complaining. Go to sleep.
George: Even the coffee tasted like plastic.
Alice: Yes, dear. Like plastic. (Looking at Matilde) She's crying again, poor dear.
George: Who?
Alice: The Colombian girl. Go to sleep.

PART NINE

Jim: (Stopping in the aisle and looking at George Hess) Excuse me. Aren't you Mr. Hess?
George: Why, yes. I don't think I . . .
Jim: You own the hardware store in Princeton, right? Don't you remember me? My name is Jim Turner.
George: Turner? Oh, are you Allan Turner's boy?
Jim: No. He's my uncle.
George: That's right. For goodness' sake. Imagine meeting here! I remember your uncle well. He was a customer of mine for twenty years or more. I'm retired now. My son-in-law runs the store. Excuse me. This is my wife, Mrs. Hess.
Jim: Nice to meet you, ma'am.
Alice: Hello, Jim.
Jim: (To George) I liked your store. I liked walking down the aisles and handling the tools.
George: Yes. I miss the place sometimes.
Alice: Now, George, you have a basement full of tools.
George: It's not the same.
Alice: (To Jim) Where are you living?
Jim: I'm going back to the States. I'm going to college in the fall.
George: How's your uncle's boy? What's his name?
Jim: Ross. He's fine.
George: He's a fine boy. And your uncle?
Jim: He's . . . (There is a terrible noise, and the plane begins to shake.) What's that? What's happening? (The plane starts to fall.) What is it?
George: I don't know. Better get to your seat.

FASTEN SEAT BELTS. FASTEN SEAT BELTS. FASTEN SEAT BELTS. FASTEN SEAT . . .

Work with the dialogue.

1. Listen to your teacher or to other Americans read the dialogues. Listen to the sounds.

2. Get into groups of three and four. Act out the dialogues for the class.

   Part Seven

Student 1:	The Director	Student 3:	George
	Jim	Student 4:	Jay
Student 2:	Abel		

   Part Eight

Student 1:	Alice	Student 3:	George
Student 2:	The Director		

   Part Nine

Student 1:	Jim	Student 3:	The Director
Student 2:	George	Student 4:	Alice

3. Get into groups of four. Play with the dialogue.

   a. Change Jim in Part Seven to Mr. Martin, a businessman. Change Abel to Mr. Chase, an ESL teacher. Mr. Martin is from England. The two men are flying from Spain to New York. Make small talk for five minutes. Use your imagination. Act out your new dialogue for the class.
   b. In Part Nine, change Mr. Hess's occupation from owner of a hardware store to owner of a liquor store. Use your imagination. Act out your new dialogue for the class.

Use the English you know—role-play.

Get into groups of five. Choose two students to be the actors.

Situation 1: Two people meet on the street.

   Student 1: Excuse me, aren't you _____?
   Student 2: Why, yes. I don't think I know you, do I?

Continue the conversation. Find out how you know the other person. Talk about what you are doing now. Talk about other people both of you know. Look at Part Nine for ideas.

Situation 2: You and a friend went to a wonderful party last night. You're talking on the phone.

   Student 1: Hello, Carmen?
   Student 2: Hello, Maria.
   Student 1: Wasn't that a wonderful party last night?
   Student 2: Yeah, it was a lot of fun.

Continue the conversation. Talk about what was fun. Talk about the people, the food, and the music at the party. Have fun!

Situation 3: You and a friend are eating dinner in a restaurant. The food is terrible.

   Student 1: This is terrible.
   Student 2: Ssh! People are listening.

Continue the conversation. Look at Part Eight for ideas.

Use the English you know—be yourself.

Situation 1:   Get into groups of three. You're at a Christmas party for ESL students at school. Student 1 is an American. Students 2 and 3 are from other countries.

    Student 1:   Are you from Latin America?
    Student 2:   How did you know?
    Student 1:   Your accent.
    Student 3:   (to Student 2) What are you studying?

Continue the conversation. Discuss: What are Students 2 and 3 studying? Why are they studying it? What questions do they have about school or life in the United States?

Extend your vocabulary.

Get into groups of two. It's okay to use your dictionary.

Two students are talking.

    Student 1:   Sometimes I miss my country.
    Student 2:   You have a good life here.
    Student 1:   Yes . . . but . . .

Continue the conversation. Talk about the things you miss and how life in the United States is different from life in your former home.

11 What Do I Have to Do to Learn English?

Read this dialogue with your teacher.

Mr. Chase: Saturday. I love Saturdays. Nothing to do.
Mrs. Chase: Come on, Milton. You have a lot to do today.
Mr. Chase: Don't I ever get a chance to rest?
Mrs. Chase: Sure, when you're eighty.

Look at this information.

Mr. Chase's Schedule

Saturday	
10:00	Take Carrie to dentist.
	Buy groceries. Get 2 qts. milk, bread, wine.
12:00	Take car to Al's Gas Station for oil change and tuneup.
3:00	Tennis with Bill in Roosevelt Park.
5:00	Pick up car.
7:00	Susan and Jay's for dinner. (DON'T FORGET WINE.)

How to Say It

> CARRIE HAS TO GO TO THE DENTIST AT 10:00.
>
> I HAVE TO BUY GROCERIES ON THE WAY HOME.

Did you notice?

	OBLIGATION		
	MODAL AUXILIARY	MAIN VERB	
Carrie	has to	go	to the dentist.
I	have to	buy	groceries.

How about a little practice?

Look at Mr. Chase's Saturday schedule. Make three more statements about what he has to do.

1. He has to _____ .
2. He has to _____ .
3. He _____ .

How about a little more practice?

Tell your classmates three things you have to do this week.

1. I have to _____ .
2. I _____ .
3. _____ .

Read this dialogue with your teacher.

(Karim and Hussein are speaking in Arabic. This is a translation.)

Karim: Hi, Hussein. How are you?
Hussein: Fine. Hey, Karim. I want to talk to you about something.
Karim: Sure. What?
Hussein: I want to speak good English—like you.
Karim: Yeah?
Hussein: What can I do?
Karim: You can go to night school. . . .
Hussein: Where?
Karim: Try McKinley High. It's free.
Hussein: Free? Is it any good?
Karim: Sure. I went there. I learned a lot. What have you got to lose?
Hussein: Nothing, I guess. . . . What do I have to do?
Karim: Register. That's it.
Hussein: Can you do that for me?
Karim: No, you have to do it.
Hussein: Anything else?

Karim: You have to take a test.
Hussein: A test? Oh, no! I hate tests.
Karim: Don't worry. It's nothing.
Hussein: Do I have to buy any books?
Karim: Buy a notebook and a dictionary. You don't have to buy anything else.
Hussein: Karim . . . uh . . . Maybe you can take the test for me.
Karim: Do you want to learn English or don't you?
Hussein: I guess so. Is it easy?
Karim: Well, you have to study and go to class.
Hussein: I don't know. . . . I didn't have to work to learn Arabic.
Karim: Hey, Hussein . . .
Hussein: Okay, okay.

Did you notice?

1.

		OBLIGATION/NECESSITY				
QUESTION	What	do	I		have to	do?
STATEMENT			You		have to	take	a test.

		NO OBLIGATION/NO NECESSITY				
STATEMENT			You / I	don't / didn't	have to / have to	buy / work	anything else. / to learn Arabic.

2.

HAVE TO	+	BASE FORM
have to		study

How about a little practice?

The drawings on p. 121 show what you have to do to get a driver's license. Look at them (or at Visual Aids #s 58–63).

120

FILL OUT an application 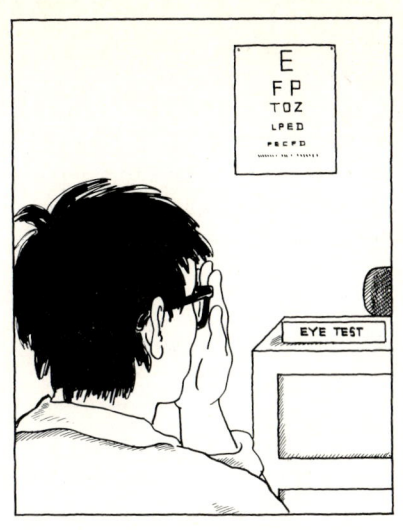   TAKE an eye test 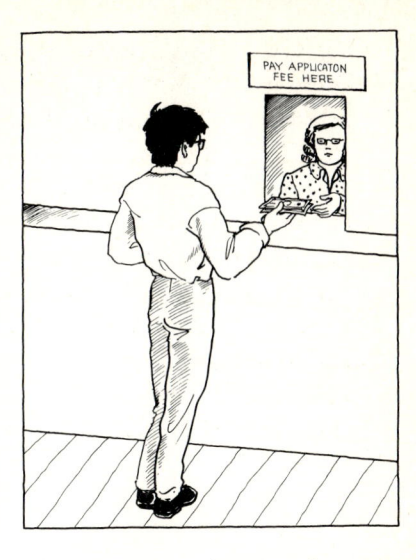   PAY an application fee

SHOW proof of age    TAKE a written test (and)    TAKE a driving test

For two students: ask about and tell what you have to do to get a driver's license.

    Student 1:   What do you have to do to get a driver's license?
    Student 2:   You have to _____.

For a group of five students: practice reporting factual information.

Choose from this list. It's okay to use your dictionary.

What do you have to do to

    get a car loan   wash a baby
    rent an apartment   get a money order
    get a job   open a savings account

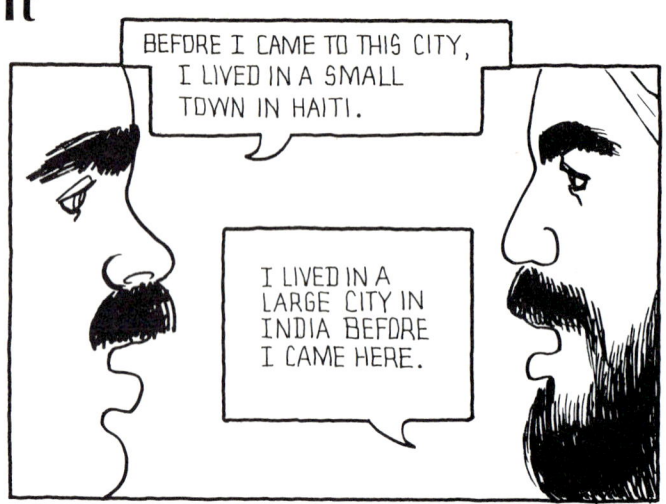

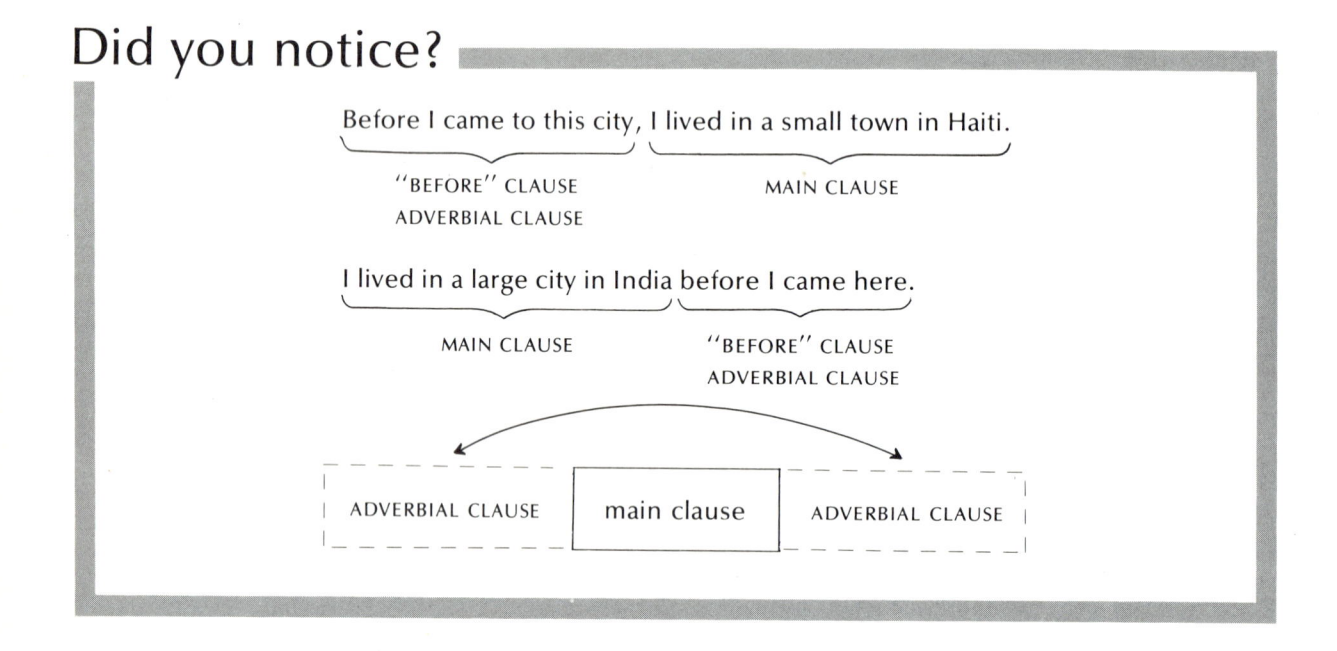

How to Say It

> BEFORE I CAME TO THIS CITY, I LIVED IN A SMALL TOWN IN HAITI.

> I LIVED IN A LARGE CITY IN INDIA BEFORE I CAME HERE.

Did you notice?

Before I came to this city, I lived in a small town in Haiti.

"BEFORE" CLAUSE / ADVERBIAL CLAUSE — MAIN CLAUSE

I lived in a large city in India before I came here.

MAIN CLAUSE — "BEFORE" CLAUSE / ADVERBIAL CLAUSE

ADVERBIAL CLAUSE — main clause — ADVERBIAL CLAUSE

How to Say It

> WHAT DID YOU DO BEFORE YOU CAME TO SCHOOL TODAY, CARMEN?

> I ATE DINNER WITH MY FAMILY.

> WHAT DID YOU DO, PIERRE?

> I DID MY HOMEWORK.

Did you notice?

```
           MAIN CLAUSE      ADVERBIAL CLAUSE
         ⎡           ⎤    ⎡                    ⎤
          What did you do before you came to school?

            QUESTION             STATEMENT
             FORM                   FORM
          (PAST TENSE)          (PAST TENSE)
```

For two students: ask and answer.

Student 1: What did you do before you ate dinner last night?
Student 2: _____
Student 1: What did you do before you came to the United States?
Student 2: _____

Language Game: The Psychology Game

Finish these sentences quickly. Use the simple present tense.

1. Before I speak English, _____.
2. Before I go to sleep at night, _____.
3. I sometimes feel sick before _____.
4. I think very carefully before _____.
5. I close my eyes before _____.

How to Say It

> BEFORE I GO TO BED, I DRINK A GLASS OF WINE.

Did you notice?

Before I go to bed, I drink a glass of wine.
                           ↑   ↑

Study this vocabulary.

a box   a can   a jar

a bag   a carton   a bottle

Language Game: The Consumer Game

Example:

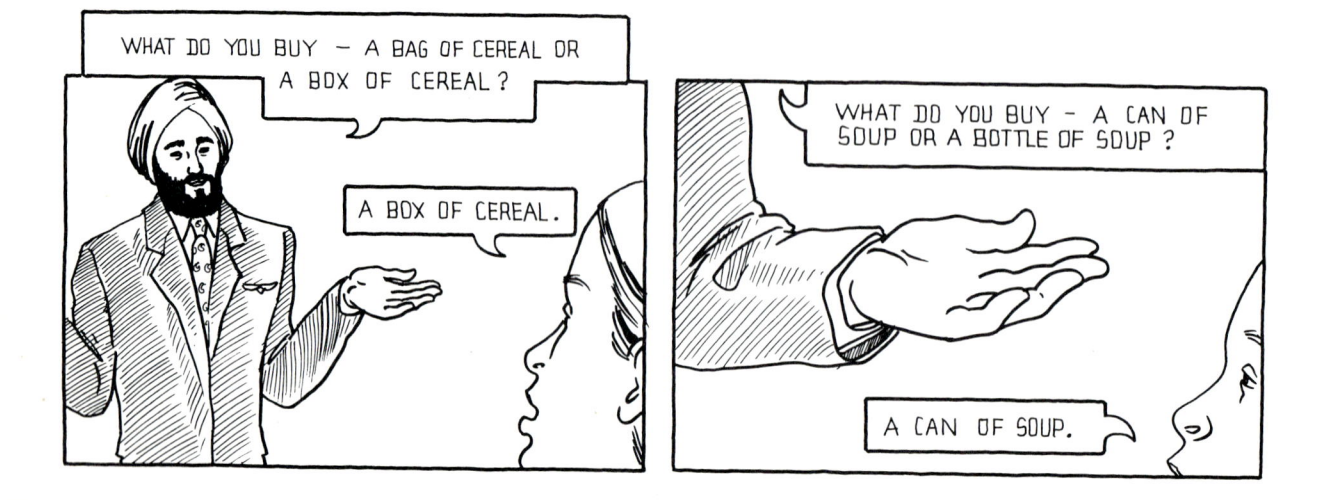

WHAT DO YOU BUY — A BAG OF CEREAL OR A BOX OF CEREAL?

A BOX OF CEREAL.

WHAT DO YOU BUY — A CAN OF SOUP OR A BOTTLE OF SOUP?

A CAN OF SOUP.

For two students: tell what you usually buy. All answers are correct. Use these words and phrases.

orange juice	a carton/a can
milk	a carton/a bottle
candy	a box/a bag
soap	a box/a bottle
coffee	a bag/a can/a jar

Student 1: What do you usually buy, _____ or _____?
Student 2: _____

Read this dialogue with your teacher.

Susan: Carmen, why did you come to New York?
Carmen: Because I wanted a better job and earn a lot of money.
Susan: Uh-huh. And you, Iqbal?
Iqbal: I want to learn computer technology.
Susan: Why?
Iqbal: So I can get a better job when I go back to India.

Did you notice?

Why did you come to New York?
Because I wanted a better job.

For two students: ask and answer.

Student 1: Why did you come to the United States?
Student 2: _____

Language Game: The Psychology Game

Finish these sentences quickly.

1. I like to go to parties because _____.
2. I want to learn English because _____.
3. I don't like to get angry because _____.
4. I hate English sometimes because _____.
5. Sometimes I want to go back to my country because _____.

How to Say It

Tatiana
5'5"
155 lbs.
49 yrs.

Fusako
5'1"
105 lbs.
21 yrs.

Tatiana is **taller**, **heavier**, and **older** than Fusako.

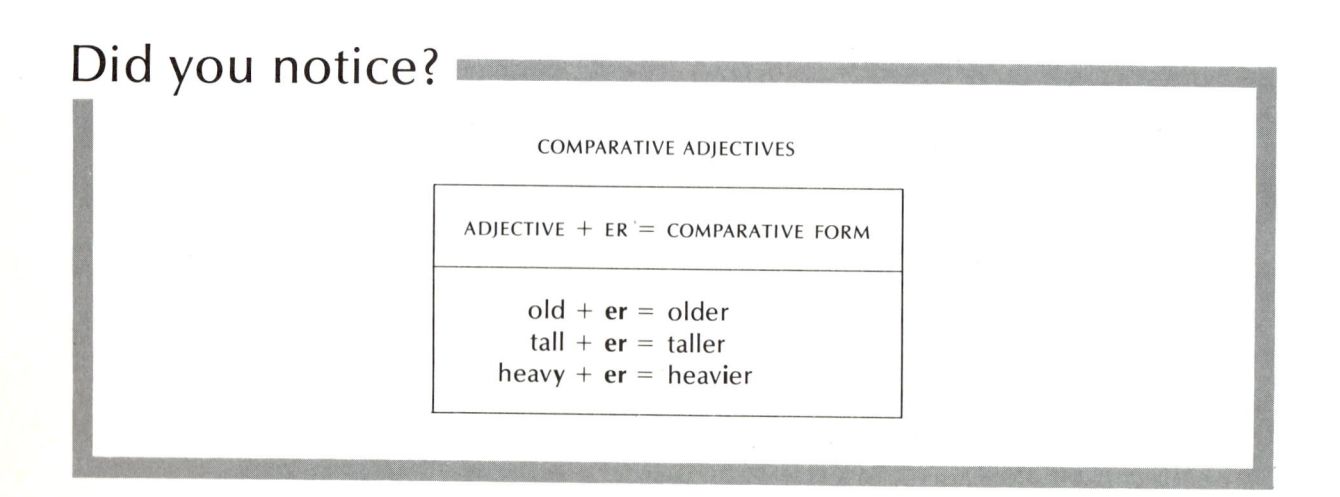

Did you notice?

COMPARATIVE ADJECTIVES

ADJECTIVE + ER = COMPARATIVE FORM

old + **er** = older
tall + **er** = taller
heavy + **er** = heavier

Practice saying these sentences.

    Tatiana is taller than Fusako.
    She's heavier.
    She's older.

How about a little practice?

Look at these drawings.

Mrs. Popov's building
   four stories
   eight apartments

Mr. Kim's building
   six stories
   eighteen apartments

Compare the buildings. Use these phrases: taller than, larger than.

    Mr. Kim's building is _____ Mrs. Popov's.

Compare two students in class.

Use these phrases: taller than, younger than, bigger than.

Compare two teachers.

Use these words: taller, older, bigger.

How to Say It

THE SPANISH BOOK IS MORE EXPENSIVE THAN THE FRENCH BOOK.

Did you notice?

MORE + ADJECTIVE

more   expensive

Do you see the difference?

more beau-ti-ful
    1 2 3

more ex-pen-sive
    1 2 3

heav-i-er
1 2 3

tall-er
1 2

How about a little practice?

Compare two cities that you know.

Example: I think Paris is more beautiful than New York.

Use these words.

    beautiful   dangerous
    expensive   interesting

How to Say It

THE POPOVS HAVE MORE CHILDREN, AND THEIR CHILDREN ARE OLDER.

Did you notice?

MORE + NOUN
more children

How about a little practice?

1. Compare these two apartments. Use **more**.

Apartment 302	Apartment 105
5 rooms	7 rooms
$320/month	$410/month
6 closets	5 closets

2. Compare the contents of these women's purses. Use **more**.

Tatiana Popov's Purse	Sophie Karkosza's Purse
1 comb	1 driver's license
6 keys	5 credit cards
3 credit cards	$36.15
1 wallet	1 voter registration card
1 brush	5 keys
$18.75	1 comb
1 driver's license	2 store coupons
	6 pictures
	1 wallet

12 No Loitering

Look at this information.

(Or look at Visual Aids #s 64–70.)

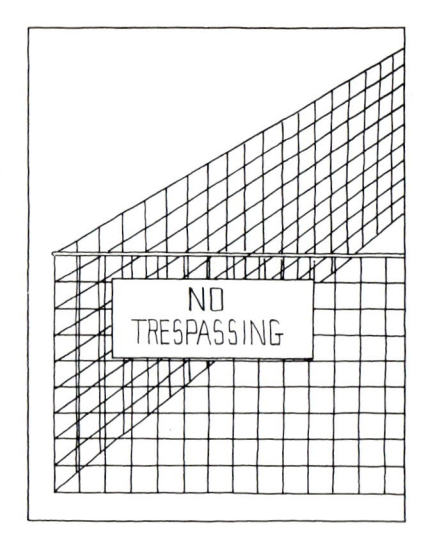

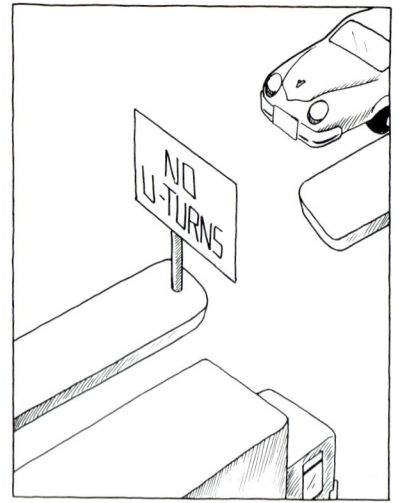

Practice saying these phrases.

No Gas
No U-turn
No Passengers
No Parking
No Loitering
No Smoking
No Trespassing

Did you notice?

1. | NO + NOUN |
    |---|
    | No   Gas |
    | No   U-turn |

2. | NO + VERB + ING |
    |---|
    | No   Parking |

How about a little practice?

Example:

Student 1: Where do you see "No Loitering" signs?
Student 2: On the street or on buildings.

For two students: ask and answer questions about signs. Look at the signs on pp. 131–132 (or at Visual Aids #s 64–70).

    Student 1:   Where do you see _____ signs?
    Student 2:   _____

How to Say It

Practice saying these sentences.

    Would you like some coffee?
    That would be nice.
    Cream, but no sugar.
    Sugar, but no milk.

Study these language functions.

	FORMAL → → →			INFORMAL
INVITING	Would you like some coffee? or Would you like to have some coffee?	Do you want some coffee?		Coffee?
ACCEPTING	That would be nice.	Yes, thank you.		Sure. Thanks.

For two students: ask and answer.

    Student 1:   Would you like _____ ?
                   or
                   Do you want _____ ?
    Student 2:   _____

Use this information.

tea	hamburger
milk	relish
sugar	mustard
lemon	ketchup
cream	onions

hot dog	pizza
mustard	cheese
ketchup	sausage
relish	onions
onions	mushrooms

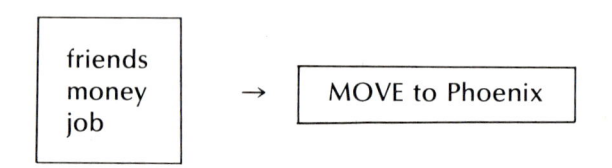

Language Game: The Pits

Example:

    Student 1:   You know, Sandra just came back from a trip. She had a terrible time. The first night she stayed at this terrible hotel.
    Student 2:   Really?

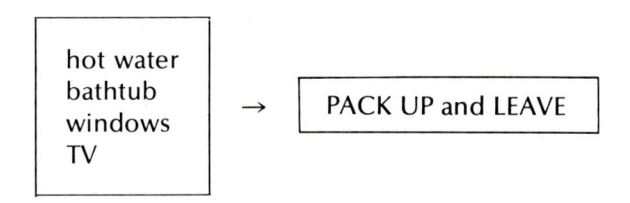

```
┌──────────┐       ┌──────────────────┐
│ hot water│       │                  │
│ bathtub  │  →    │ PACK UP and LEAVE│
│ windows  │       │                  │
│ TV       │       └──────────────────┘
└──────────┘
```

Student 1:   There was **no hot water, no bathtub** . . .
Student 2:   That's terrible.
Student 1:   . . . **no windows, no TV,** . . . nothing.
Student 2:   What did she do?
Student 1:   She **packed up** and **left.**

For two students: Student 1, tell Student 2 about Sandra. Use the information in the boxes.

1. Student 1:   Sandra had a terrible vacation.
   Student 2:   Really?

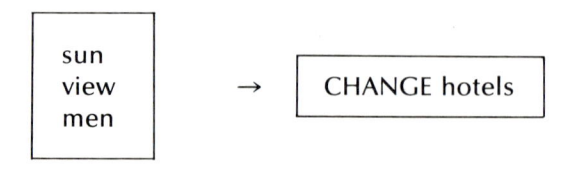

```
┌──────┐       ┌──────────────┐
│ sun  │       │              │
│ view │  →    │ CHANGE hotels│
│ men  │       │              │
└──────┘       └──────────────┘
```

2. Student 1:   Sandra was very unhappy last year.
   Student 2:   Really?

```
┌────────┐       ┌──────────────────┐
│ friends│       │                  │
│ money  │  →    │ MOVE to Phoenix  │
│ job    │       │                  │
└────────┘       └──────────────────┘
```

3. Student 1: Sandra went to a terrible party.
   Student 2: Really?

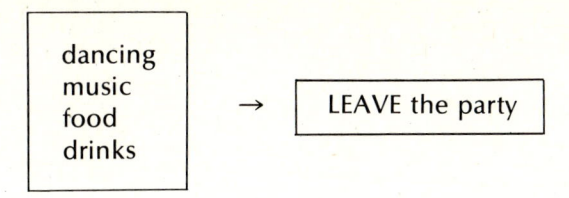

   | dancing
   music
   food
   drinks | → | LEAVE the party |

Language Game: The Heights

Example:

   Student 1: Everyone wants to live in a good neighborhood. What does that mean—a good neighborhood?

   | nice
   clean
   crime
   noise |

   Student 2: It's **nice** and **clean**. **No crime** and **no noise** at night.
   Student 1: I agree.

For two students: Student 1, ask another student for his or her opinion. Student 2, make positive statements and negative statements using the words in the boxes.

1. Student 1: Everyone wants to have a happy life. What does that mean—a happy life?

   | good friends
   sickness
   money problems
   nice children |

2. Student 1: Everyone wants to have a nice weekend. What does that mean—a nice weekend?

   | party
   dinner
   family problems
   rain
   good movie |

3. Student 1: Everyone wants to have a good ESL course. What does that mean—a good ESL course?

   | good teacher
   tests
   homework
   nice classmates |

How to Say It

> IN CHINA, MOST OF THE PEOPLE GO TO WORK ON BICYCLES. BUT IN LOS ANGELES, THEY DRIVE TO WORK.

> IN ITALY, MANY PEOPLE GO HOME FOR LUNCH. BUT IN NEW YORK CITY, PRACTICALLY NO ONE DOES.

Did you notice?

all of the people	100%
most of the people	more than 50%
no one	0%

many people	a large number of people
some people	a number of people

How about a little practice?

Compare your country and the United States. Use **many people, most of the people, all of the people, no one, some people.**

Student: In _____, _____ people _____ _____. But in the United States, _____ _____.

Here are some ideas.

1. Compare the time people go to bed.
2. Compare the time people go to work.
3. Compare the kinds of cars people drive.
4. Compare the things people do on their days off.
5. Compare the kinds of clothes people wear to school.
6. Compare the number of children people have.
7. Compare the kinds of food people eat for breakfast.

Read this conversation with your teacher.

Pierre: How do you make instant coffee?
Sophie: Easy. **First** you get some water, and you put it in a pot. **Then** you put the pot on the stove. You boil the water. You put one spoon of instant coffee in the cup. You pour the boiling water into the cup. Then you put in milk and sugar, and you stir the coffee. **Then** you drink it.

Sophie used these words.

VERBS	NOUNS	
get	water	cup
put in	spoon	milk
boil	pot	coffee
pour	stove	sugar
stir		
drink		

Practice saying these sentences.

First you get some water.
Then you put the pot on the stove.
You put one spoon of instant coffee in the cup.
Then you pour water into the cup.
Then you drink it.

For two students: ask and answer.

1. Student 1: How do you make a pot of tea?
   Student 2: _____

   Use these words.

VERBS	NOUNS
get	tea
put in	pot
boil	spoon
wait	stove
pour	cup
stir	milk
drink	sugar
	lemon

2. Student 1: How do you use a washing machine?
   Student 2: _____

   Use these words.

VERBS	NOUNS
separate	washing machine
open	white clothes
put in	colored clothes
close	detergent
start	
take out	

3. Student 1: How do you start a car?
   Student 2: _____

Use these words.

VERBS	NOUNS
open	car
get in	door
put the car in neutral (N)	key
put the car in park (P)	ignition
put in	gas pedal
turn	clutch
step on	

4. Student 1: How do you open the door of your house or apartment?
   Student 2: _____

Use these words.

VERBS	NOUNS
get out	door
put in	key
turn	knob
push/pull	lock

How to Say It

WHEN JOSÉ FIRST CAME TO THE U.S., HE DIDN'T KNOW HOW TO SPEAK ENGLISH. HE GOT LOST THREE TIMES AND DIDN'T KNOW HOW TO ASK FOR HELP.

Did you notice?

	SUBJECT		MAIN VERB PAST FORM	
STATEMENT	I		knew	how to speak Spanish.

	SUBJECT	NEGATIVE PAST FORM	MAIN VERB BASE FORM	
NEGATIVE STATEMENT	I	did + not didn't	know	how to speak English.

QUESTION WORD + INFINITIVE				
	TO	+	BASE FORM	
how how	to to		ask speak	for help English

Practice saying these sentences.

 He didn't know how to speak English.
 He didn't know how to ask for help.

Read this dialogue with your teacher.

 Steve Kern: When I went to Mexico, I didn't know how to buy a bus ticket. When I went to Italy, I didn't know how to use a public phone. You learn a lot when you travel.
 Soo Ho Kim: Yes. When I came here, I didn't know how to take a bus.
 Steve Kern: Uh-huh. What did you do?
 Soo Ho Kim: I went to a bus stop, got on a bus and watched the people in front of me. I put some money in my hand and showed the money to the driver. He took two quarters and put them in the machine. That's how I learned.

For two students: ask and answer.

 Student 1: What did you have to learn when you came to the United States?
 Student 2: I didn't know how to _____ .
 Student 1: How did you learn?
 Student 2: _____

How to Say It

> WHAT'S THE MATTER WITH HER?
> SHE DOESN'T KNOW WHERE SHE IS.
> WHERE AM I?

Did you notice?

QUESTION		Where	am	I?	
STATEMENT	She doesn't know	where		she	is.

Practice saying these sentences.

What's the matter with her?
She doesn't know where she is.
Where am I?

How to Say It

> WHERE DID YOU GO LAST NIGHT?
> TO A MOVIE WITH SEVENTEEN BEAUTIFUL WOMEN!
> JOSÉ,...
> WHY CAN'T I HAVE SOME PRIVACY?

> WHAT HAPPENED? WHY IS YOUR FATHER ANGRY?
>
> HE WANTED TO KNOW WHERE I WENT LAST NIGHT.
>
> AND?
>
> I DIDN'T TELL HIM.

Did you notice?

QUESTION		Where	did	you	go	last night?
STATEMENT	He wanted to know	where		I	went	last night.

How about a little practice?

Look at this story.

Monday

> WHY DID YOU SMILE AT THAT WOMAN?

141

Tuesday

"WHO DID YOU CALL?"

Saturday

"WHY DID YOU DANCE WITH FUSAKO THREE TIMES?"

Yesterday

"HEY! WHO DID YOU GET INTO THAT TAXI WITH LAST NIGHT?"

For two students: ask and answer questions about Carmen's week.

How to Say It

> WHY IS HE TAKING HIS SHOES TO THE REPAIR SHOP?

MAYBE HE NEEDS TO GET HIS SHOES REPAIRED OR POLISHED.

NOUN	VERB
shoes	repair polish

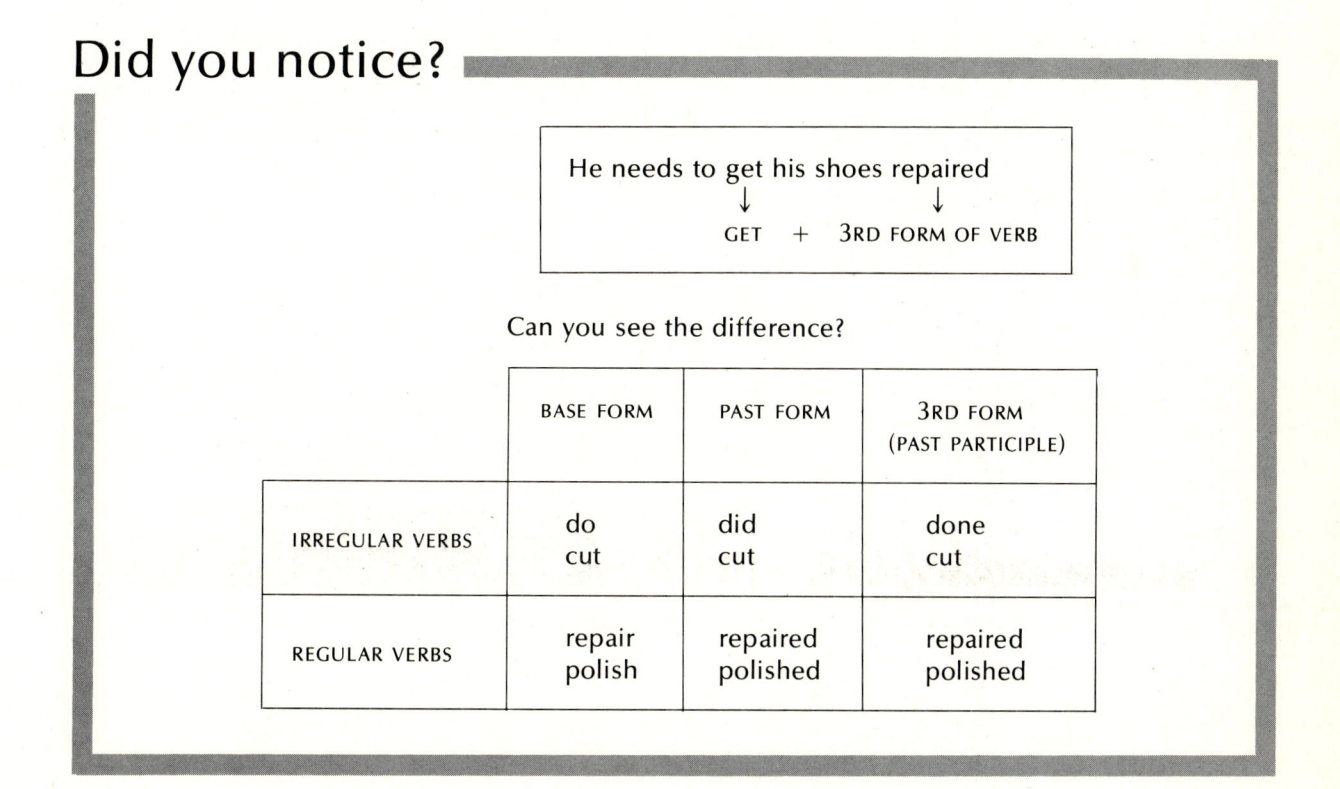

Did you notice?

He needs to get his shoes repaired
↓   ↓
GET   +   3RD FORM OF VERB

Can you see the difference?

	BASE FORM	PAST FORM	3RD FORM (PAST PARTICIPLE)
IRREGULAR VERBS	do cut	did cut	done cut
REGULAR VERBS	repair polish	repaired polished	repaired polished

Practice saying these sentences.

    He needs to get his shoes repaired.
    He needs to get them polished.

How about a little practice?

For two students: ask and answer.

1. Student 1: Why is he taking his car to the garage?
   Student 2: Maybe he needs to get _____ .

NOUN	VERB
car	fix
oil	change
engine	tune up
tires	change

2. Student 1: Why is she calling a plumber?
   Student 2: Maybe _____ .

NOUN	VERB
sink	fix
shower	fix

3. Student 1: Why is she going to the beauty parlor?
   Student 2: Maybe she wants _____.

NOUN	VERB
hair	do
hair	cut
nails	do

4. Student 1: Why is he going to the dry cleaners?
   Student 2: _____.

NOUN	VERB
coat	clean
sweater	repair
pants	

145

Read this story by yourself.
Then read it with your teacher.

Flight 18

PART TEN

	(Everyone is listening.)
The Captain:	This is your Captain speaking. We have an emergency. Return to your seats. Obey the seat belt and no smoking signs.
	(The plane is falling. Everyone is talking. Some people are starting to panic. Jim returns to his seat.)
Abel:	I'm glad you got back. What's happening?
Jim:	I don't know.
Abel:	Is the plane falling? Are we going to crash?
Jim:	I don't know.
	(The plane continues to fall. Two people start screaming and crying. The flight attendant tries to calm them.)
Abel:	Where are we? Are we over water?
Jim:	I think that's the coast down there. Oh, God. (Jim starts to cry.) I don't want to die. I'm too young to die.
Abel:	Whatever happens is God's will.
Jim:	(Looking out the window) We're still falling. (Crying) No, we can't. (To Abel) What's the matter with you? Aren't you scared?
Abel:	(Calmly) It's God's will.
Kathy:	(In a very calm voice) Please remain calm. The plane is losing altitude, but the captain's in control. Please be calm.
Alice:	The flight attendant. She's doing a good job. (Turning to George) My dear, what do we do?
George:	Nothing. (He takes her hand and kisses it.) My dear, I don't regret anything. I don't want to leave you. Maybe this is a good way. We had a good life. We were never sick a day, and we are going together. Be brave, Alice, dear.
Alice:	Oh, George, you're a wonderful man. Hold me. Don't let me go.

Kathy:	Ladies and gentlemen. We are at 15,000 feet. We are talking to the Coast Guard. And we are preparing to make an emergency landing in the ocean. We are about twenty miles off the coast of North Carolina. The weather is fine and the sea is calm. Please be calm and listen for emergency landing instructions.
Jim:	Emergency landing instructions! What a laugh. We're going to crash. The plane is out of control. How can he land? We're going to crash and die and that's that. Why doesn't he just tell us the truth? We probably have only a few minutes to live—maybe less. Damn it! Damn it! (Jim sobs.)
Abel:	Don't curse. (Abel holds Jim's arm.) Thank God.

PART ELEVEN

Kathy:	Is your seat belt fastened, sir? Miss?
Jay:	(To Kathy) Why don't you sit down?
Kathy:	We're going to be all right. (To Matilde) Miss, is your seat belt fastened?
Matilde:	Yes, thank you. (To Jay) How can she be so calm? It's funny, now I can't cry.
Jay:	It's strange. I went to Colombia because my mother was sick—maybe dying—and now . . . Susan is pretty and still young. She can get married again. And my little boys . . .
Matilde:	Don't cry.

PART TWELVE

The Captain:	This is your Captain. We're all right. We are no longer losing altitude. We are at 5000 feet and steady. We will be landing at Norfolk International Airport in Norfolk, Virginia, in fifteen minutes. Please stay seated and do not smoke.
Jim:	It's true. It's true. Look! (Jim sobs with relief. Other people in the plane are laughing and cheering.)
Abel:	Jim. (He puts his arm over Jim's shoulder.) Jim, we're okay. (Jim continues to sob.) We're okay. (He stops Kathy as she is going by.) You did a fine job. I admire you.
Kathy:	Thank you.
Abel:	I know you have a lot of people to take care of, but can you bring my friend a drink?
Kathy:	I'll try. (She goes away.)
Abel:	Jim?

(Jim doesn't answer. He looks away from Abel. Abel looks toward the back of the plane.)

Abel:	Jim, the flight attendant is coming with a drink. Here. Take it.
	(Jim takes the drink and says nothing.)

PART THIRTEEN

George:	Well, my dear, I guess it wasn't our time to go, after all.
Alice:	And a good thing, too. I still have lots of things to do and lots of places to see. (They laugh.) Look at that ocean, and the sky and the clouds. It's all so beautiful.
George:	I'm glad to be alive. I'm not really brave, you know. I just wanted to be brave for you.
Alice:	Me too. (They laugh again.)

PART FOURTEEN

Abel:	Jim? Are you all right?
Jim:	Leave me alone.

Kathy:	(To Abel) Is he all right?
Abel:	Uh . . . He isn't feeling very well.
Jim:	(Yelling at Abel) You don't have to make excuses for me!
Abel:	I'm sorry.
Kathy:	(To Jim) Can I help you?
Jim:	No. No, thank you. (Jim and Abel sit in silence for a while.) I'm sorry, Abel. Really. I acted like a . . .
Abel:	Don't apologize, Jim. I understand.
Jim:	No, you don't. I'm a coward, no guts. I'm a fake. I'm a loudmouth. And I'm a . . .
Abel:	Jim, we're all afraid to die.
Jim:	You weren't.
Abel:	Of course, I was.
Jim:	Maybe so.

PART FIFTEEN

Jay:	You know, nothing is more important than the people you love. Money, all those other things—they're nothing. Oh no, you aren't crying again, are you?
Matilde:	Yes.
Jay:	Why?
Matilde:	I'm happy, happy to be alive.

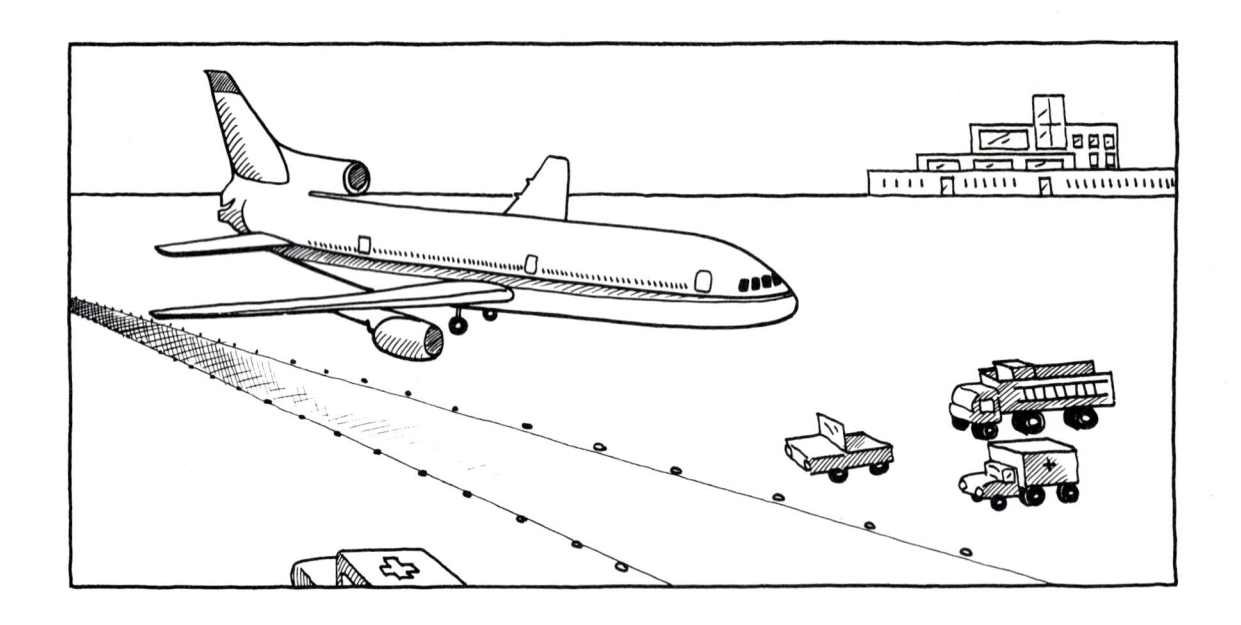

Work with the dialogue.

1. Listen to your teacher or other Americans read the dialogues. Listen to the sounds.

2. Get into groups of three and six. Act out the dialogues for the class.

   Parts Ten, Twelve, Thirteen, and Fourteen

Student 1:	The Director		Student 4:	Kathy
	The Captain		Student 5:	Alice
Student 2:	Abel		Student 6:	George
Student 3:	Jim			

Parts Eleven and Fifteen

Student 1:	Kathy	Student 2:	Jay
	The Director	Student 3:	Matilde

3. Get into groups of six. Play with the dialogue.

   a. In Part Ten, change "We have an emergency" to "We're having some turbulence."
   b. Change "The plane is falling" to "The plane is bouncing up and down."
   c. Change Jim's words "I don't want to die" to "I don't want to get sick."

Continue the dialogue. Act out your new dialogue for the class.

Get into groups of two. In Part Fourteen, start the conversation:

Jim: You don't have to make excuses for me!
Abel: Now wait a minute. I'm tired of this. Grow up.

Continue the conversation. Act out your new dialogue for the class.

Use the English you know—role-play.

Get into groups of five. Choose two students to be the actors.

Situation: A young husband and wife are talking.

Student 1: We never have any fun anymore.
Student 2: What do you mean?
Student 1: I work two jobs. It's shoes this week. Your teeth last week. Money, money, money.

Continue the conversation. Student 2, try to calm down Student 1. Look at Part Ten (George and Alice) and Part Fourteen (Jim and Abel) for ideas.

Use the English you know—be yourself.

Situation 1: Two students are talking.

Student 1: I'm never going to learn English. I hate this class.
Student 2: Sure you can. Our teacher is doing a good job.

Continue the conversation. Talk about all your feelings.

Situation 2: Two friends are talking.

Student 1: It's a beautiful day.
Student 2: You sound happy.

Continue the conversation. Talk about good feelings.

Extend your vocabulary.

Get into groups of four. Tell your classmates about an accident with a car, a bus, a bicycle, or an airplane. As you tell your story, your classmates should ask you questions or show sympathy (for example: "That's too bad" "How awful!" "Oh!"). It's okay to use your dictionary.

13 He Won't Eat Carrots

Read this dialogue with your teacher.

(Carmen and Maria are speaking Spanish. This is a translation.)

Carmen:	Hello?
Maria:	Hello, Carmen?
Carmen:	Maria?
Maria:	Yes. Oh, Carmen, what am I going to do?
Carmen:	What's the matter?
Maria:	I just got my telephone bill.
Carmen:	Yes.
Maria:	It's $120.
Carmen:	What?
Maria:	I didn't make all these calls. Here's one to Pittsburgh. I don't even know anyone in Pittsburgh.
Carmen:	Don't worry about it.
Maria:	What can I do? I can't pay $120. I don't have $120.
Carmen:	Go down to the phone company on Monday.
Maria:	I work.
Carmen:	You can call them.
Maria:	You know I hate to speak English over the phone.
Carmen:	Write them a letter.
Maria:	I hate writing English even more.
Carmen:	Well, Maria, I don't know what to suggest.

Maria: Do you think there is someone who speaks Spanish at the phone company?
Carmen: Probably. Call and ask.
Maria: Good idea. Thanks.
Carmen: Tell me what happens.
Maria: Okay. Thanks, Carmen. Bye.
Carmen: Yeah, bye.

Did you notice?

What can I do? Do you know any foreign languages?
You *can* call them. I *can* speak Spanish.
↓ ↓
POSSIBILITY ABILITY

Practice saying these sentences.

What can I do?
You can call them.
I can't pay $120.

How about a little practice?

Look at these drawings and discuss some **possibilities** with your classmates. Use **can**. You can use your dictionary or ask your teacher for help.

1. What can he do?

"YOU KNOW, I ALWAYS GET LOST IN THIS CITY. ALL THE STREETS LOOK THE SAME TO ME. AND WHEN I ASK FOR DIRECTIONS, PEOPLE ALWAYS SAY, "HUH? WHAT DID YOU SAY?""

2. What can Mrs. Kim do?

> I'M SORRY, MRS. KIM. YOU HAVE TO MOVE! NO BABIES ALLOWED IN THIS BUILDING.
>
> BUT MY BABY IS ONLY ONE WEEK OLD!
>
> I'M SORRY. YOU HAVE TO MOVE OUT BY FRIDAY.

3. What can he do?

COLOR T.V. FOR SALE THIS WEEK ONLY!! WAS $590 NOW ONLY $477

I REALLY WANT THAT TV, BUT I DON'T HAVE $477.

4. What can José do?

> WHAT ARE YOU HAVING, FRANCESCA?
>
> STEAK. AND YOU?

BOB'S RESTAURANT

STEAK	8.95
CHICKEN	4.50
ROAST BEEF	8.5
HAM	6.0
SHRIMP	7.
HAMBURGER	3.

> STEAK? OH, BOY. UH... LET'S SEE. STEAK IS $8.95. MAYBE SHE THINKS I'M RICH. I ONLY HAVE $20 AND WE HAVE TO HAVE COFFEE. AND I HAVE TO TAKE HER HOME....

How to Say It

Did you notice?

1.
VERY GOOD	It was very good.
↓	It was good.
↓	It was pretty good.
↓	It was pretty bad.
↓	It was bad.
VERY BAD	It was very bad.

2. If they *call* this week, *I'll tell* them.
   ↓ ↓
   PRESENT FORM   FUTURE FORM

FUTURE FORM
WILL + BASE FORM
will	tell

I	will
I'll	

←a contraction

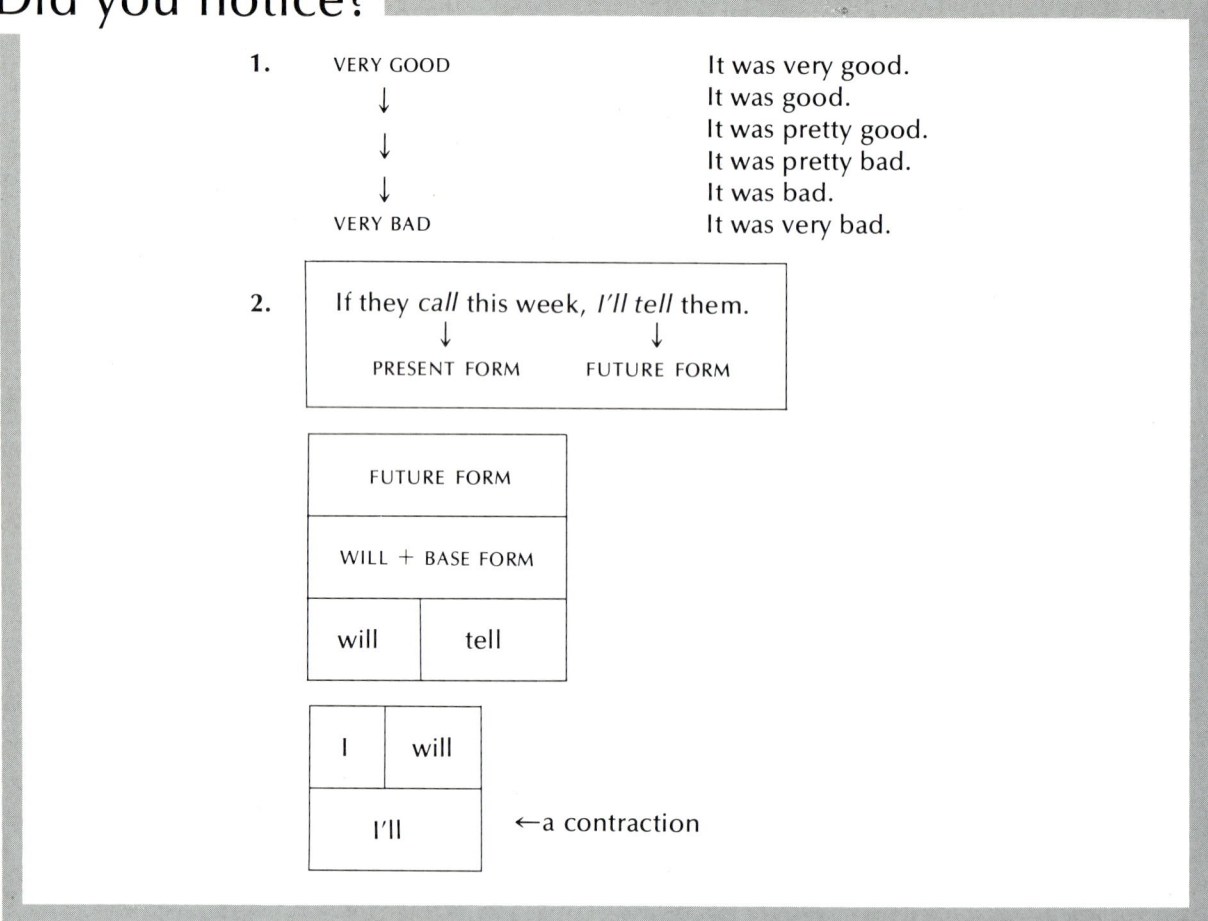

Practice saying these sentences.

I heard about your accident.
It was pretty bad.
Did you tell your parents?
No. But if they call this week, I'll tell them.

How to Say It

DID YOU SEE PIERRE TODAY?

NO. WHY?

I WANT TO TALK TO HIM.

I'LL TELL HIM IF I SEE HIM.

THANKS.

Did you notice?

```
    ┌─────────┐                    ┌─────────┐
    │"IF"     │   ┌──────────┐    │"IF"     │
    │CLAUSE   │   │MAIN CLAUSE│   │CLAUSE   │
    └─────────┘   └──────────┘    └─────────┘
```
If I see him, I'll tell him.
　　　　　　　I'll tell him if I see him.

Practice saying these sentences.

　　I want to talk to him.
　　I'll tell him if I see him.

Language Game: The Psychology Game

Finish these sentences quickly.

Example: If I get sick, I'll go to see a doctor.

1. If it rains tomorrow, _____.
2. If I take a vacation, _____.
3. If I have $100, _____.
4. If we have lunch together, _____.
5. If I get a new job, _____.

Finish these sentences quickly.

Example: I'll get a new car if I have to fix my old car again.

1. I'll get angry if _____.
2. I'll go to the airport if _____.
3. I'll laugh if _____.
4. My friend's boss will not be happy if _____.
5. I'll go to bed at 7:00 P.M. if _____.

Read this paragraph with your teacher.

Nikolai is a man of strong opinions. When he says he won't do something, he won't do it. Here are some of the things he won't do.

　　He won't dance.
　　He won't eat carrots.
　　He won't swim in the ocean.
　　He won't cook.
　　He won't stay in bed after 8:00 A.M.

Did you notice?

will	not
won't	←a contraction

Practice saying these sentences.

He won't dance.
He won't eat carrots.
He won't swim in the ocean.
He won't cook.
He won't stay in bed after 8:00 A.M.

How about a little practice?

Example:

I WON'T EAT LIVER.

A LOT OF PEOPLE DON'T LIKE IT.

I WON'T GET MARRIED THIS YEAR.

YOU WON'T? WHY NOT?

I DON'T KNOW ANYONE I WANT TO MARRY AND I DON'T HAVE ENOUGH MONEY.

I CAN UNDERSTAND THAT!

For two students.

    Student 1:   Tell a classmate four things you won't do.
    Student 2:   Respond to Student 1.
    Student 1:   Answer, if you want to.

How about a little more practice?

Tell your classmates four things you think you'll do this week. (Use "will.")

Example: I think I'll go to the bank this afternoon.

How to Say It

How about a little practice?

1.

For two students: ask and answer. Look at the pictures (or use Visual Aids #s 71–75).

Student 1: What do you think will happen next?
Student 2: They'll probably _____ .

2.

Student 1: What do you think will happen next?
Student 2: He'll probably _____ .

3.

Student 1: _____
Student 2: _____

4.

"WHAT HAPPENED?"
"WAH!"

Student 1: _____
Student 2: _____

5.

"YOUR HOMEWORK IS ALL WRONG."
"I CAN'T BELIEVE IT!"

Student 1: _____
Student 2: _____

How to Say It

"WHAT ARE YOU GOING TO DO AFTER WORK TOMORROW?"
"I'M GOING TO GET MY HAIR DONE. WHY?"
"I WANT TO GO SHOPPING."
"CAN'T YOU GO ALONE?"
"IT'S MORE FUN IF I HAVE COMPANY."
"I KNOW HOW YOU FEEL."

Did you notice?

QUESTION	What	are	you		going to	do	tomorrow?
STATEMENT			I	am	going to	get	my hair done.

FUTURE FORM

AM
ARE + GOING TO + BASE FORM
IS

I	am	going to	get	my hair done.

How about a little practice?

For two students: ask and answer.

1. Student 1: What are you going to do after class?
   Student 2: _____

2. Student 1: What are you going to eat for dinner tonight?
   Student 2: _____

3. Student 1: Who are you going to see this weekend?
   Student 2: _____

How about a little more practice?

For two students: ask and answer questions about the future.

Example:

    Name two sports teams.
    Ask, "Who _____ win?"

    Student 1: The Cowboys and the Eagles are playing tomorrow. Who is going to win?
    Student 2: The Cowboys.
    Student 1: Why?
    Student 2: They're bigger and faster.
    Student 1: Oh.

1. Name two sports teams.
   Ask, "Who _____ win the championship?"
2. Name two political candidates.
   Ask, "Who _____ win the election?"

3. Name a problem in the news.
   Ask, "What _____ happen?"
4. Name something that changes price (gas, food, clothing, etc.).
   Ask, "What _____ happen to the price of _____?"
5. Name a person in the news (a famous person, an actor, an actress, a criminal).
   Ask, "What _____?"

**Read this story by yourself.
Then read it with your teacher.**

Flight 18

PART SIXTEEN

(At the Norfolk airport, the passengers are waiting for another plane to take them to New York.)

Jay:	(Seeing George in the crowd) How are you? Pretty exciting trip.
George:	A little too exciting. (Turning to Alice) This is my wife, Alice.
Jay:	Jay, Jay Gutierrez.
George:	George Hess. (They shake hands.)
Alice:	Hello, Jay. Well . . . now what?
Jay:	That's a good question.
George:	What do you think happened?
Jay:	I don't know. There was a bang. You heard it, right? And then the plane started to fall.
George:	Yeah.
Jay:	They say most accidents happen at takeoff and landing, but . . .
Alice:	Well, this one sure didn't, did it?
Jay:	Hey, there's the flight attendant. (Calling to her) Hello, there.
Kathy:	Hi.
Jay:	You were great, just great. (People cheer, applaud, and shake hands with her.) You deserve a medal.
Kathy:	Oh, no. It's my job . . . but thank you, anyway.

Alice:	You're a brave woman. What's your name? I'm going to write to the president of the airline and tell him about the fine job you and the others did.
Kathy:	No, really, I just . . .
Alice:	No, you deserve recognition. (Everybody agrees. Some applaud.) Tell us your name.
Kathy:	Kathy Vandenberg.
George:	Miss Vandenberg, can you tell us what happened?
Kathy:	I don't know, really. Maybe the Captain can.
Abel:	Excuse me, are we going to get another plane to New York?
Kathy:	Yes, I'm sure they'll have one for you as soon as possible.
Jim:	Do we have to take a plane?
Kathy:	Uh . . . I don't know. The airline has to get you to New York if you want to go.
Jim:	Listen, I don't want to go up in a plane again. No way. I'm sorry. Not me.
	(Silence, everyone looking at Jim)
Kathy:	I understand.
Alice:	Let's not bother Miss Vandenberg. She's not responsible.
A Young Woman:	But he has a point. I don't want to get into another plane either. Not for a long, long time. We almost got killed, you know.
Jim:	Can we talk to someone?
Kathy:	Certainly. I'll call the supervisor. (Kathy leaves.)
A Businessman:	I have to get to New York as soon as possible. I have a flight to Brussels in four hours.
Matilde:	My mother is waiting for me in New York—she is probably hysterical right now.
Jay:	Wait a minute! Wait a minute! Let's vote. How many people **don't** want to take the plane to New York? (He counts the hands.) About fifteen or twenty. The rest want to get to New York as soon as possible, right? Okay. Look! Here's the Captain. (To the Captain) Thank you. Thank you very much. We owe you our lives. (Everyone applauds.) What happened? Can you tell us?
The Captain:	I'm sorry. We can't discuss it. But don't worry, there'll be a full investigation. They'll probably ask some of you to testify.
Alice:	You did a fine job, and I'll tell them so. I'm sure we're here because of you. (Everyone agrees.) Ah . . . Captain? Some of us don't want to take another plane. Not today.
The Captain:	I understand. I'm sure the airline will help you. But . . . ah, you know a limousine or a bus to New York will probably take seven or eight hours.
Matilde:	(To Jay) Ask him when the plane to New York is leaving.
Jay:	Sir, when is the plane leaving?
The Captain:	I think they're getting it ready now. You can probably board in about twenty minutes.
Jay:	You're not coming?
The Captain:	No, I have to make a report. It'll take hours to finish. Believe me, folks, don't worry. The chances of this happening again are a million to one. Okay? Well, I have to go. Good luck to you all.
Jay:	Yeah, thanks again.
	(Everyone thanks him again.)
George:	Well, Abel and Matilde, welcome to the United States. You certainly came in with a bang!
Alice:	George Hess! That's not funny.

Work with the dialogue.

1. Listen to your teacher or other Americans read the dialogue. Listen to the sounds.

2. Act out the dialogue for the class. Select one student to be the Director and one student to be each of the characters.

Jay	Jim
George	A Young Woman
Alice	A Businessman
Kathy	Matilde
Abel	The Captain

Use the English you know—role-play.

Get into groups of five.

Situation 1: You were riding in a plane. It had to land because of engine trouble.

Student 1: Can you tell us what happened?
Student 2: (flight attendant) I don't know, really.
Student 3: Are we getting another plane?
Student 4: I don't want to go up in a plane, ever.

Continue the conversation. Try to get information from the flight attendant. Discuss the problem with the other passengers. Discuss the passengers' fear of flying. Discuss other ways of getting home.

Situation 2: A mother and father are waiting at the airport for their daughter. Their daughter's flight is going to be two or three hours late. They know the plane has had engine trouble.

Student 1 (father): I hope everything is all right.
Student 2 (mother): They never tell you anything, do they?

Continue the conversation. Talk about your fears. Discuss how to get more information from the airline.

Use the English you know—be yourself.

Get into groups of four. Choose two people to be the actors.

Situation: You want to thank a friend. Your friend did something very nice for you.

Student 1: _____, I want to thank you so much. You were great.
Student 2: It was my pleasure.
Student 1: No, really. You were wonderful.

Continue the conversation. Talk about what your friend did for you.

14 I'm Talking to Myself More These Days

Read this dialogue with your teacher.

Sophie: Did you find an apartment?
Tatiana: No, we're still looking.
Sophie: Really?
Tatiana: We looked at two on Saturday.
Sophie: Didn't you like them?

Tatiana: One had six rooms. It was too expensive.
Sophie: Uh-huh.
Tatiana: The other was too small for us.
Sophie: Too bad.

Did you notice?

It was **too** expensive.
  (The Popovs **cannot** afford it.)
The other was **too** small.
  (It does **not** have enough space.)
Too is a negative word when we use it in front of adjectives like this.

How about a little practice?

What's the matter here? Make statements. Use **too**.

Example:

The shirt's too big.

The pants are too small.

1.

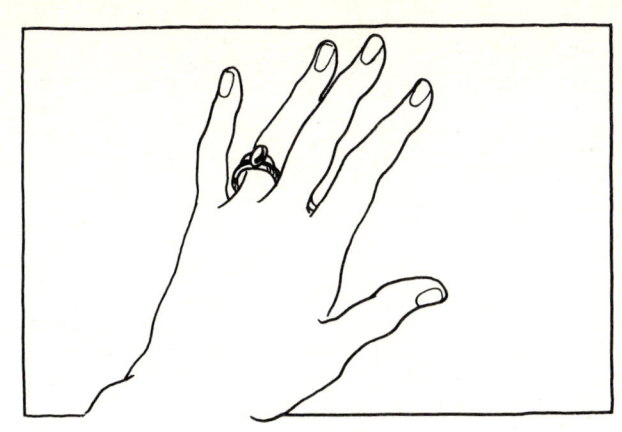

2.
WE WANT TO PAY ABOUT $250.
I LOVE IT!
SORRY. THIS APARTMENT IS $400.

3.
IT'S 96°. I CAN'T WORK! 

4.
DO YOU WANT TO DANCE? 
BUT, YOU'RE 6'5"!

5.
WOULD YOU LIKE TO BUY THIS DIAMOND RING?
HOW MUCH?
$25.
$25 FOR A DIAMOND? ARE YOU KIDDING?

Language Game: The Psychology Game

Finish the following sentences quickly.

Example: Too much coffee can make you ___nervous___ .

1. Too much candy can make you _____ .
2. Too much liquor can make you _____ .
3. Too much money can make you _____ .
4. Too much noise can make you _____ .
5. Too much English can make you _____ .

How to Say It

(Look at Visual Aids #s 76–79.)

While   WALK to work,   TRIP

and   FALL.   But   BE okay.

Milton: What happened to Wen Yu this morning, Maria?
Maria: **While** he **was walking** to work, he **tripped** and **fell**. But it was all right. He was okay.

Did you notice?

	PAST PROGRESSIVE	
	WAS WERE	BASE FORM + ING
He	was	walking	to work.

How about a little practice?

1. These drawings show what happened to Fusako at the department store. Look at them (or at Visual Aids #s 80–82).

While

SHOP for dresses,

SEE.

But when

TRY ON.

For two students: ask about and tell what happened to Fusako at the department store.

Student 1: What happened to Fusako?
Student 2: While _____.

167

2. These drawings show what happened to Karim last night. Look at them (or at Visual Aids #s 83–87).

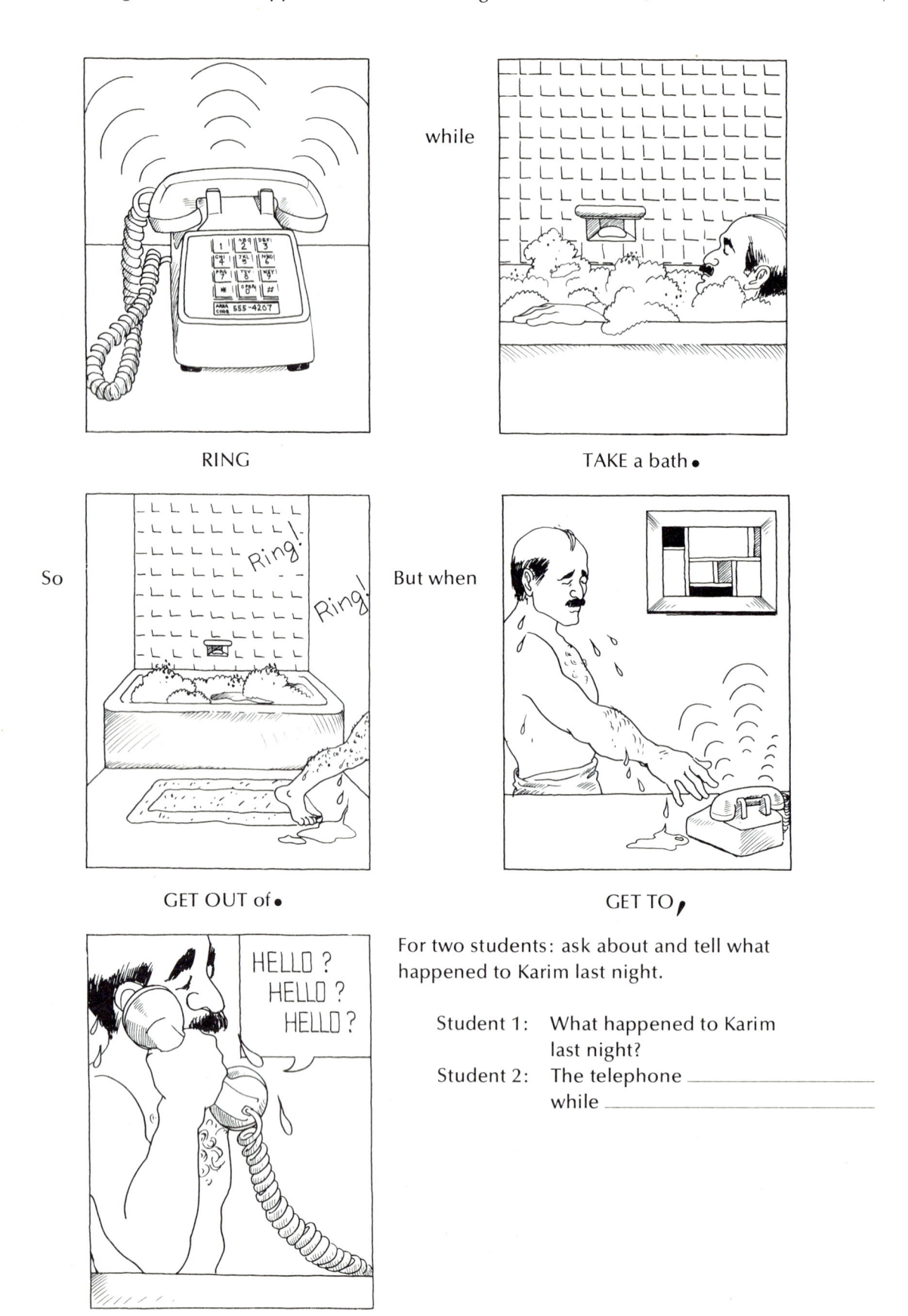

RING

while

TAKE a bath.

So

GET OUT of.

But when

GET TO,

For two students: ask about and tell what happened to Karim last night.

Student 1: What happened to Karim last night?
Student 2: The telephone _____ while _____

168

3. These drawings show what happened to Susan on the way to work this morning. Look at them (or at Visual Aids #s 88–99).

While

DRIVE to work,

GET.

A FLAT TIRE. DARN IT!

So

WALK

and

HELLO, EMERGENCY SERVICE?

CALL.

I HAVE A FLAT TIRE.

TELL.

WHAT? ONE HOUR?

TELL.

169

So

GO back.

STOP.

PUT ON,

While

WAIT,

DO YOU NEED HELP?

and

ASK.

THANK YOU! THANK YOU SO MUCH. HAPPY TO HELP.

and

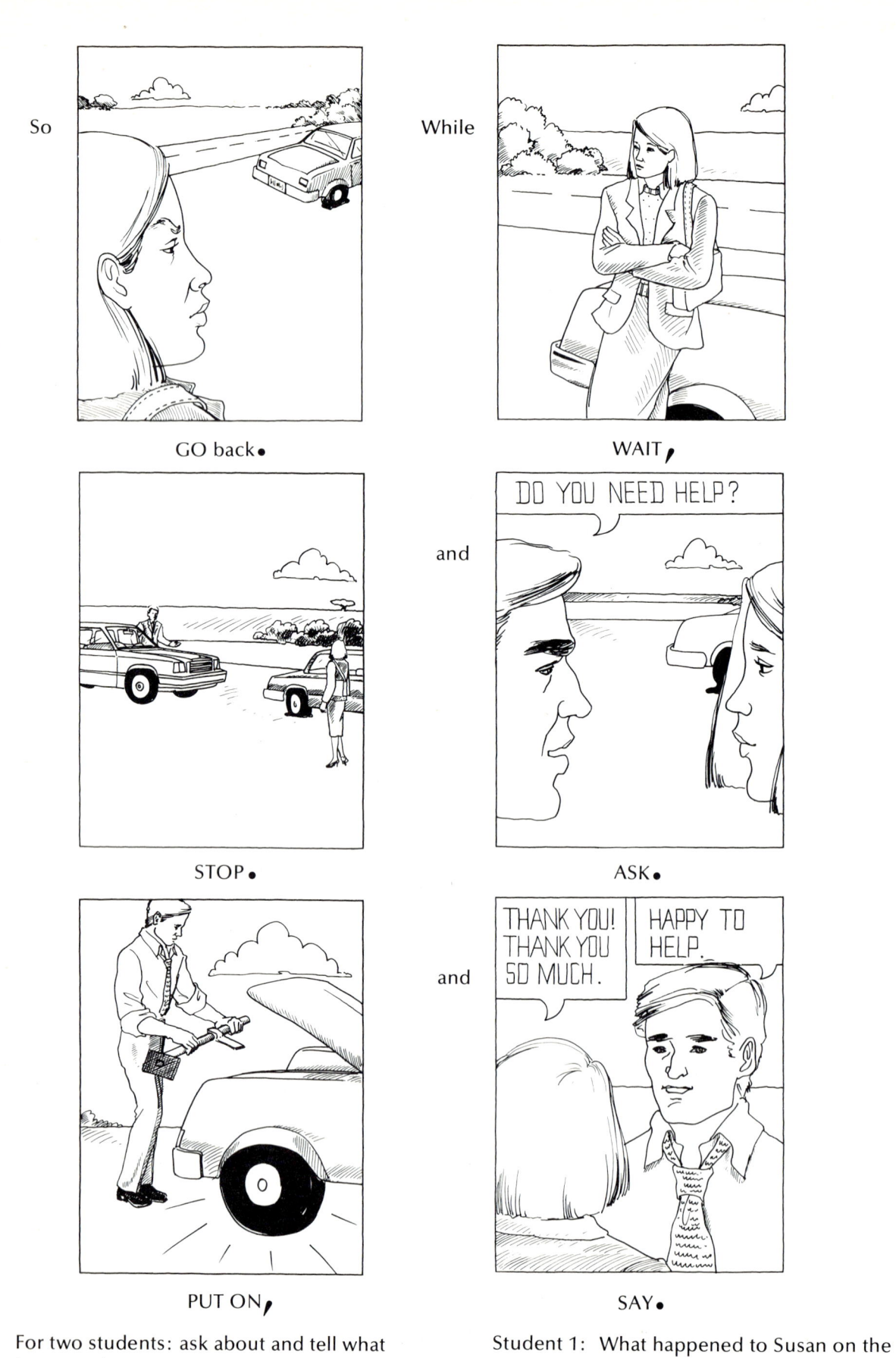

SAY.

For two students: ask about and tell what happened to Susan on the way to work this morning.

Student 1: What happened to Susan on the way to work this morning?
Student 2: While _____.

170

Study this grammar.

COMPARATIVE	SUPERLATIVE
taller **more** expensive	**the** tallest **the most** expensive

Read this list with your teacher.

The longest rivers
   The Amazon and the Nile are more than 3000 miles long.

The largest ocean
   The Pacific is almost 64,000,000 square miles in area.

The highest mountain
   Mt. Everest is more than 29,000 feet high.

The tallest people
   The Watutsi (Tutsi) of Rwanda and Burundi in Africa are the tallest people in the world. The men average 6'1".

The most intelligent person
   Kim Ung-Yong of Seoul, South Korea, has an I.Q. of 210. He was born in 1963.

The fastest English speaker
   In 1961, John Kennedy spoke 327 words in one minute.

The best language learner
   Sir John Bowring (1792–1872) spoke 100 languages and read two hundred.

The most complicated languages
   Chippewa, a North American Indian language, has about 6000 verb forms.
   The Eskimo language has 63 forms in the present tense.

The most difficult sentence in English to say fast.
   The sixth sheik's sixth sheep's sick.

How about a little practice?

For three students: Look at the following and guess what superlative you can use with them.

Example: whale _____ the largest animal in the ocean _____

1. elephant _____
2. Alaska _____
3. Rhode Island _____
4. Soviet Union _____
5. New York City _____
6. China _____
7. London _____

Study this grammar.

	IRREGULAR COMPARATIVES	SUPERLATIVES
	better than farther than worse than	the best the farthest the worst

How about a little more practice?

Make some statements about your family or about people you know. Use **superlatives.** You can use some of these words.

old   nice   young   pretty   tall   handsome   intelligent   successful

Example:

FLORENCE IS THE OLDEST AND I AM THE YOUNGEST CHILD IN THE FAMILY. WE THINK MY BROTHER JOHN IS THE MOST INTELLIGENT. HE GOT THE BEST GRADES IN SCHOOL. BUT MY BROTHER KEVIN IS THE MOST SUCCESSFUL. HE'S AN ACCOUNTANT AND MAKES A LOT OF MONEY.

How to Say It

OUCH!

She cut **herself.**

DAMN!

He hit **himself.**

Study this grammar.

POSSESSIVE ADJECTIVE	REFLEXIVE PRONOUN
my	myself
your	yourself
her	herself
its	itself
our	ourselves
your	yourselves
his	* himself
their	* themselves

* irregular

How about a little practice?

Look at the pictures. Answer the question. Use reflexive pronouns.

Example:

What's the baby girl doing?
(look at)
She's looking at herself.

1. What's José doing?
(talk to)

2. What's he doing? (time)

3. What are they doing? (watch)

How about a little more practice?

For two students: Tell each other about things that have happened to you or to people you know. Use reflexive pronouns. You can use some of these verbs, if you want to.

cut	hit	hurt	listen to	teach
like	hear	ask	talk to	see

Example: The first time I heard myself on tape I was really surprised. I sounded very young.

**Read this story by yourself.
Then read it with your teacher.**

Flight 18

PART SEVENTEEN

Jim: I guess I have to make up my mind.

Abel: Take the plane, Jim. Then you can show me around New York. We can go to a movie or just walk around.

Jim: Your uncle is meeting you at the airport?

Abel: Yes. You'll like him.

Jim: You'll have a lot of things to talk about. I'll just be in the way.

Abel: No, no. My uncle isn't like that. You're my only American friend. I don't want to lose you now.

Jim: (Turns to the Hesses) Excuse me. How are you getting home?

Alice: We're taking the plane. Our daughter and son-in-law are meeting us at the airport. Do you need a ride to Princeton?

Jim: Uh . . . gee. That's really nice of you. My uncle doesn't know I'm coming and . . .

Alice: Well, we'll be happy to give you a ride.

Jim: Thank you. (Turns back to Abel)

Abel: Jim, you still don't look like you're sure. Don't worry. The plane will be all right. Believe me.

Jim: I know. You're probably right.

Abel: What's that expression in English? When you fall off a horse, . . .

Jim: . . . you should get right back on. I know, I know. All right. I'll take the plane.

Abel: Good.

PART EIGHTEEN

Matilde: I know my mother's upset.

Jay: Huh?

Matilde: I want to call her at the airport. Do you think I can?

Jay: Probably, but I'll bet they already know what happened. Everyone in the country probably knows by now.

Matilde: I hope my mother does. She doesn't speak English very well. She probably won't understand the announcements.

Jay: Don't worry. I told you—lots of people speak Spanish in New York. Someone will tell her.

Matilde: I guess you're right. You spoke very well in front of those people. Your English was wonderful.

Jay: It wasn't always so good.

Matilde: How did you learn?

Jay: I went to school at night. That's where I met my wife.

Matilde: You met her at school?

Jay: Yeah. I learned a lot of English in school, but it doesn't hurt to fall in love with an English teacher!

Matilde: You met her at night school? Oh, that's romantic.

Jay: Yes. I guess it is. We were young. I was very handsome then. I had all my hair.

Matilde: Oh, come on. You aren't that old.

Jay: I'm 39. That's old enough. Anyway, after we got married, I spoke English all the time. The kids don't know any Spanish except for a few words. That's the way it is. And then, you know, on the job I speak English.

Matilde: What do you do, may I ask?

Jay: I work for Con Ed. That's the gas and electric company in New York. It's a good job. Good pay. Good benefits. Lots of overtime, two weeks vacation. And I like the guys I work with. Sure the job has problems—every job has problems. But it's okay. And when I retire, I won't have to worry about a thing. Maybe we'll move to Florida and buy a house near the beach. That's the life, you know—clean air and sunshine.

Matilde: Sounds wonderful. Is it hard to get a job with your company?

Jay: Nah. They hire all the time. And they want to hire women and minority people.

Matilde: Why?

Jay: The government says so.

Matilde: Do you think I could get a job with Con Ed?

Jay: Do you have a high school diploma?

Matilde: Yes, but I don't know anything about gas and . . .

Jay: That's all right, they'll train you.

Matilde: It's hard to believe.

Jay: Yeah, but that's America—the "land of milk and honey." Listen, call the Personnel Office and . . . No, don't do that. Let me talk to some people first. Call me next week and I'll have the information for you.

Matilde: Really? You'll do that for me?

Jay: Sure. Why not?

Matilde: But I'm a stranger.

Jay: Listen, you'll learn. Things happen fast in America. I like you, so we're friends.

Matilde: I don't have your phone number.

Jay: Oh, right. It's 555 . . .

Matilde: Wait. Let me find a piece of paper . . . okay . . .

Jay: 555–0101.

Matilde: 555–0101. Thank you. I'm really excited. Maybe it'll be all right after all.

Jay: Sure. It's a great country. You can do anything you want, be anything you want. The sky's the limit. My kids are going to have all the things I didn't have. They're going to go to college and . . . be like that kid over there. (Looks at Jim)

Matilde: Oh, I hope not. I don't like him.

Jay: Oh? Did you talk to him?

Matilde: No, but I can tell.

Jay: (He laughs.) He seems like a nice kid.

Matilde: Hmm. I can't wait to see my parents.

Jay: You feel better about things now?

Matilde:	Yes, a lot better.
Jay:	I want you to meet Susan and the children when we land.
Matilde:	Jay?
Jay:	Mmmm?
Matilde:	Is your wife very jealous?
Jay:	What?
Matilde:	If you introduce me . . . and I have your phone number . . .
Jay:	(He smiles.) No. She trusts me.
Matilde:	Yes? That's strange.
Jay:	You're in for a lot of surprises.

Work with the dialogue.

1. Listen to your teacher or other Americans read the dialogues. Listen to the sounds.

2. Get into groups of three and four. Act out the dialogues for the class.

   Part Seventeen:

Student 1:	The Director	Student 3:	Abel
Student 2:	Jim	Student 4:	Alice

   Part Eighteen:

Student 1:	Jay	Student 3:	Matilde
Student 2:	The Director		

3. Play with the dialogue.

   a. Get into groups of six. In Part Seventeen, change "Take the plane, Jim" to "I don't care. Stay here and take a bus to New York." Continue the dialogue. Act out your new dialogue for the class.

   b. Get into groups of four. In Part Eighteen, change "I work for Con Ed" to "I work in a factory that makes buttons. It isn't a very good job." Continue the conversation. Act out your new dialogue for the class.

   c. Get into groups of six. In Part Eighteen, change "Is your wife very jealous?" "No" to "Is your wife very jealous?" "Yes." Continue the conversation. Act out the new dialogue for the class.

Use the English you know—role-play.

Get into groups of five. Choose two students to be the actors.

Situation 1: One student asks another for help in finding a job.

Student 1:	I need a job.
Student 2:	What kind of job are you looking for?
Student 1:	Well, I _____ .

Continue the conversation. Decide: what kind of job you want; where you can look for more information; who you can ask for help or introductions.

Situation 2:	You are thinking about retirement. You decide to talk about it with your family. You live in Chicago.

Student 1 (husband):	When I retire, we'll probably move to Florida.
Student 2 (wife):	Florida? I don't want to go so far away.
Student 3 (son):	I don't want to go to Florida. It's too hot.
Student 1:	Well, I don't want to stay around here. The winters are too cold and the summers are too hot.

Continue the conversation. Decide: where you want to live when you retire; what you don't like about where you are living now; what you like and don't like about other parts of the United States or the rest of the world.

Use the English you know—be yourself.

Get into groups of four. Have two students be the actors.

Situation 1:   Your children do not want to speak your native language. Your friends have the same problem with their children.

Student 1:   _____ and _____ don't want to speak _____ anymore. (Use the names of your children and your language.) I think they are forgetting everything they learned.
Student 2:   My children are the same.
Student 1:   What can we do about it?

Continue the conversation. Discuss what you can do and how much you have to accept. Discuss how you feel about the situation.

Situation 2:   You have dreams for your children or for the children you may have in the future.

Student 1:   My kids are going to have a better life than I have had.
Student 2:   Oh yeah? What's going to be different?

Continue the conversation. Discuss: the things you want for your children; the things you had when you were a child.

Extend your vocabulary.

In groups of four to six, tell your classmates about a time when your train, plane, bus, or car was delayed. As you tell your story, answer questions from other students. It's okay to use your dictionary.

15 We Should Go Out and Celebrate

How to Say It

Fusako: The Popovs invited me to dinner. Should I bring a gift?
Milton: If someone invites you to dinner, you should bring something for that person. You don't have to, but it's nice. You can bring some wine or a cake or some flowers.

Did you notice?

Advising Others to Do Something

1. SHOULD + BASE FORM

| You | should | bring | something. |

2. When you want to make a suggestion or give advice*

STRONGEST	Bring wine!
↓	You have to bring wine.
↓	You should bring wine.
↓	You can bring wine.
WEAKEST	Why don't you bring wine?

* The meaning of the verbs and verb forms can change with the situation and with the tone of voice.

Practice saying these sentences.

Go home!
You have to go home.
You should go home.
Why don't you go home?

How about a little practice?

For two students: describe a problem and practice giving advice.

Example:

> IT'S MY WIFE'S BIRTHDAY AND I DON'T KNOW WHAT TO GET HER. WHAT DO YOU THINK?
>
> WHY DON'T YOU TAKE HER TO DINNER?

take her to dinner
buy her a present
buy her flowers

1. Student 1: I'm very tired. I worked all day.
   Student 2: Why don't you _____ ?

go home to bed
sit down and relax
take a hot bath

2. Student 1: I just heard Maria was sick.
   Student 2: _____

call her
go and see her
send her a card

3. Student 1: My wife is away for a few days.
   Student 2: _____

come to my house for dinner
stay with us
go out with some old friends

4. Student 1: Darn it! It's raining again.
   Student 2: _____

stay home and relax
go shopping
go to a movie

How about a little more practice?

Give advice. Use **have to, should,** and **can.**

Example: In the United States, when someone invites you to a wedding, should you
answer the invitation or not?
bring a present or send a present?
wear good clothes or everyday clothes?

> WELL, IF YOU ASK ME, I THINK YOU SHOULD WEAR GOOD CLOTHES. YOU HAVE TO ANSWER THE INVITATION. YOU SHOULD GIVE A PRESENT, BUT YOU CAN BRING IT OR SEND IT.

1. When you go to someone's house for dinner, should you
   be on time or late?
   bring a present or not?
   wear formal clothes or regular clothes?

   ADVICE: Well, if you ask me, I think _____ .

2. When you go to someone's house for a party, should you
   be on time or late?
   bring a present?

   ADVICE: _____

3. When you go for a job interview, should you
   be on time or late?
   wear jeans or nice clothes?
   ask questions or only answer the questions they ask?

   ADVICE: _____

4. When you feel sick, should you
   call a friend or a doctor?
   take a hot bath or a cold one?
   go to a hospital or stay at home?

   ADVICE: _____

Still more practice

Here are some questions many Americans are discussing today. We have different opinions. Discuss two of the questions and give your opinions. Use **can, should,** and **have to**.

1. How many children should a man and woman have?
2. Should women hold a full-time job or stay home with the children?
3. If a wife works, should her husband do half the work in the house or should she do it all?
4. Should a company give a man time off from work when he and his wife have a baby?

How to Say It

Tatiana, 1954   Tatiana, 1980

SHE USED TO WEIGH 105 POUNDS, BUT SHE DOESN'T ANYMORE.

OKAY, LET'S SEE... CARTER, FORD, NIXON, JOHNSON, KENNEDY, EISENHOWER, UH... ROOSEVELT...UH...

HE USED TO KNOW THE NAMES OF ALL THE PRESIDENTS OF THE UNITED STATES.

Did you notice?

	USED TO	BASE FORM	
She	used to	weigh	105 pounds.

USED TO: Describes something that was true in the past but is probably not true now

Practice saying these sentences.

She used to weigh 105 pounds.
He used to know the names of all the Presidents.

How to Say It

> WHEN I WAS YOUNG, OUR FAMILY USED TO GO TO THE BEACH EVERY SUNDAY MORNING IN THE SUMMER. MOTHER MADE SANDWICHES FOR LUNCH. BUT WE USED TO EAT THEM AS SOON AS WE GOT TO THE BEACH. MY BROTHER AND I USED TO PLAY ALL DAY IN THE SUN. BUT MOTHER SAT UNDER AN UMBRELLA.

How about a little practice?

Make statements. Use **used to**.

1. Describe how you used to look.

    Example: I used to be fat.

2. Describe what you used to do on holidays in your country.

    Example: In Afghanistan, we used to go to Paghman for picnics.

3. Name a job or jobs you used to have. Describe what you did.

    Example: I used to be a salesperson. I sold magazines door-to-door.

4. Describe some bad things you used to do when you were young.

    Example: At dinner I used to kick my brother under the table. He never said anything. But when he kicked me, I used to cry and tell Mother.

5. Describe how you used to feel about the United States and Americans.

**Read this story by yourself.
Then read it with your teacher.**

Flight 18

PART NINETEEN

(The plane takes off. Jim holds onto the seat. Abel takes a quick look at Jim and then looks away. As the engines get louder, Abel puts his hand over Jim's.)

Abel: It's all right, my friend.

(Jim smiles. After the plane stops climbing, Jim slowly relaxes and Abel takes his hand away.)

Abel: (Smiling at Jim) Jim, how about teaching me some of the words they don't put in books. And you can be my guide in the jungles of New York.
Jim: The jungles of New York! (He laughs.) That's a good one! Okay, it's a deal. (He looks out the window for a moment.) Abel?
Abel: Yes?
Jim: You're a nice guy.

PART TWENTY

Alice: I hope they got our bags on the plane. I'm always afraid they are going to lose them.
George: Now, Alice, did they ever lose our bags?
Alice: No, but I'm always afraid they will.
George: What are you going to worry about next!
Alice: I hope we're on a different plane.
George: ALICE! (George and Alice laugh.)

(Alice sees Jim across the aisle and one row ahead. She leans forward in her seat to talk to him.)

Alice: Hello, Jim.
Jim: (Turning around in his seat) Hi!
George: Hello.

Jim:	Hello. Oh. Mrs. Hess . . .
Alice:	Yes.
Jim:	I want to thank you for offering me a ride to Princeton. But I'm going to stay with Abel and his uncle in New York for a day or two. I'll see you in Princeton.
Alice:	I'm glad you made a friend.
Jim:	Yes . . . . Well, thanks again. Nice meeting you both.
Alice:	Nice meeting you, too, Jim. Good luck at school.
Jim:	Thanks.

(Alice sits back and continues talking to George.)

Alice:	Now, where was I? Oh, yes. What will I serve?
George:	What?
Alice:	At the party.
George:	What party?
Alice:	At the party I'm going to have for all of us.
George:	Oh, Alice. Never a dull moment.

PART TWENTY-ONE

Jay:	(Looking down at New York) Look at that! Isn't that something? That's the greatest city in the world.
Matilde:	It's so big. I didn't know it was so big.
Jay:	You know, I really missed New York while I was back in Colombia.
Matilde:	The United States is really your country now.
Jay:	It was odd, but I really felt like a foreigner in Colombia. You're right. I'm finally an American.
Matilde:	What a trip! I'm so glad it's almost over.
Jay:	I don't know about you, but I feel like celebrating. I feel like . . .
Matilde:	My knees are shaking. That's how I feel now. My knees are shaking. But I'm so glad to be here and be alive. I want to celebrate, too.
Jay:	Matilde, you're quite a young lady.
The Flight Attendant:	Ladies and gentlemen, we are approaching La Guardia Airport. Please fasten your seat belts and extinguish all smoking material. Please put all carry-on articles under the seat in front of you and put your seat back in an upright position.
The Captain:	Ladies and gentlemen, on your left is New York Harbor and the Statue of Liberty.
Matilde:	There it is! There it is! I'm going to cry again.
The Captain:	As we make our final turn for the airport, you will see the city of New York. Tonight you can see all the way from the George Washington Bridge to Newark, New Jersey.

PART TWENTY-TWO

Jim:	Look, Abel. That's Manhattan. See the Empire State Building?
Abel:	There, I see it. It looks just like it did in *King Kong*!
Jim:	You saw *King Kong*? I didn't know they showed that movie in Africa.
Abel:	Sure. Why not?
Jim:	What a riot!
Abel:	Where's the Brooklyn Bridge?
Jim:	Over there. You can't see it too well from here.

Abel: And the United Nations?
Jim: There. See it? It's that green-glass building with the white sides.
Abel: I see it. My uncle works there.
Jim: He does?

PART TWENTY-THREE

(Alice and George are talking.)

Alice: Remember when . . .
George: I know what you're going to say. Remember when we came back from Europe in 1938 and sailed past the Statue of Liberty?
Alice: Yes. I'll never forget it. America seemed so perfect then—so free, so strong, so safe. Wars and trouble were so far away.
George: I cried, I think.
Alice: I think everybody did. Do people cry when they see the Statue of Liberty these days?
George: I don't know.
Alice: I guess they don't.

Work with the dialogue.

1. Listen to your teacher or other Americans read the dialogues. Listen to the sounds.
2. Get into groups of two to five. Act out the dialogues for the class.

   Part Nineteen

   | Student 1: | The Director | Student 3: | Jim |
   | Student 2: | Abel |

   Part Twenty

   | Student 1: | Alice | Student 3: | George |
   | Student 2: | The Director | Student 4: | Jim |

   Part Twenty-one

Student 1:	Jay	Student 4:	The Captain
Student 2:	Matilde	Student 5:	The Director
Student 3:	The Flight Attendant

   Part Twenty-two

   | Student 1: | Abel | Student 2: | Jim |

   Part Twenty-three

   | Student 1: | Alice | Student 2: | George |

3. Play with the dialogue.

   a. Get into groups of six. In Part Twenty-one, change "You know, I really missed New York while I was back in Colombia" to "Now that I am almost here, I want to go back to Colombia." Continue the conversation. Act out the dialogue for the class.
   b. Get into groups of four. In Part Twenty-two, change "There, I see it" to "I can't see out the window; what does it look like?" Continue the conversation. Act out the dialogue for the class.

Use the English you know—role-play.

Get into groups of five. Choose two students to be the actors.

Situation 1: You are returning home from vacation.

   Student 1: I don't know if I want to come home or not.
   Student 2: Of course you do.
   Student 1: I'm not so sure. I had such a wonderful time.

Continue the conversation. Try to make Student 1 feel happy to be home.

Situation 2: You are in a plane and you are going to live in Tahiti for a year. Your husband/wife is with you.

   Student 1: I am so excited.
   Student 2: Really?
   Student 1: I've dreamed about going to Tahiti since I was young.
   Student 2: It's going to be very nice.
   Student 1: Aren't you excited, too?
   Student 2: Not really.

Continue the conversation. Discuss: what you think life will be like; things you are worried about; things you are excited about.

Use the English you know—be yourself.

Get into groups of four. Choose two students to be the actors.

Situation 1: A person you know invites you to dinner on Saturday. You are going to visit a friend on that night.

    Student 1: I want to thank you for inviting me to dinner Saturday. But . . .

Continue the conversation. Look at Part Twenty for ideas. Try to make the person who invited you feel good.

Situation 2: You are in a plane circling over the city where you live.

    Student 1: Look. Do you see _____ ?
    Student 2: Oh, yes. Isn't it beautiful?

Continue the conversation. Point out famous places (mountains, rivers, buildings, parks, and so on). Describe some of the places so that Student 2 will know what you are talking about. Look at Parts Twenty-one and Twenty-two for ideas.

Situation 3: You are talking to some Americans at a party.

    Student 1: What were your first impressions of _____ ?
                                                     (your city)
    Student 2: You mean, how did I feel about it?
    Student 1: Yeah.

Continue the conversation. Student 1 is an American. Mention how you came to the city (by car, boat, etc.). Also mention the time of day and what you thought of the buildings, the people you saw, and the people you met.

Extend your vocabulary.

1. Tell your classmates about a bad experience you had on a trip. Listen to other students tell their stories. Ask questions and make comments like, "I'll bet you were angry"; "I'll bet you wanted to turn around and go home"; or "I'll bet you wanted to hit someone."

2. In groups of five, discuss how your impressions of the United States changed. Were your first impressions correct? Were some wrong? Are you happier now than you were on the day you arrived?

It's okay to use your dictionary.

Frequently Used Irregular Verbs*

BASE FORM	PAST FORM	THIRD FORM
awake	awoke	awaked/awoken
become	became	become
begin	began	begun
bend	bent	bent
bet	bet	bet
bid	bid	bidden/bid
bite	bit	bitten/bit
bleed	bled	bled
blow	blew	blown
break	broke	broken
bring	brought	brought
build	built	built
burn	burned	burned/burnt
burst	burst	burst
buy	bought	bought
catch	caught	caught
choose	chose	chosen
come	came	come
cost	cost	cost
cut	cut	cut
do	did	done
draw	drew	drawn
drink	drank	drunk
drive	drove	driven
eat	ate	eaten
fall	fell	fallen
feed	fed	fed
feel	felt	felt
fight	fought	fought

BASE FORM	PAST FORM	THIRD FORM
find	found	found
fly	flew	flown
forget	forgot	forgotten
freeze	froze	frozen
get	got	gotten
give	gave	given
go	went	gone
grow	grew	grown
hang	hung	hung
hear	heard	heard
hide	hid	hidden/hid
hit	hit	hit
hold	held	held
hurt	hurt	hurt
keep	kept	kept
know	knew	known
lay	laid	laid
lead	led	led
leave	left	left
lend	lent	lent
let	let	let
lie	lay	lain
light	lit	lit
lose	lost	lost
make	made	made
mean	meant	meant
meet	met	met
pay	paid	paid
put	put	put

* American English

BASE FORM	PAST FORM	THIRD FORM	BASE FORM	PAST FORM	THIRD FORM
quit	quit	quit	stick	stuck	stuck
			stink	stank	stunk
read	read	read	strike	struck	struck
ride	rode	ridden	swear	swore	sworn
ring	rang	rung	sweep	swept	swept
rise	rose	risen	swell	swelled	swelled/swollen
run	ran	run	swim	swam	swum
say	said	said	take	took	taken
see	saw	seen	teach	taught	taught
sell	sold	sold	tear	tore	torn
send	sent	sent	tell	told	told
shake	shook	shaken	think	thought	thought
shine	shone	shone	throw	threw	thrown
shoot	shot	shot			
shrink	shrank	shrunk	understand	understood	understood
shut	shut	shut			
sing	sang	sung	wake	woke	waked/woken
sit	sat	sat	wear	wore	worn
sleep	slept	slept	weep	wept	wept
speak	spoke	spoken	win	won	won
spend	spent	spent	wind	wound	wound
stand	stood	stood	write	wrote	written
steal	stole	stolen			